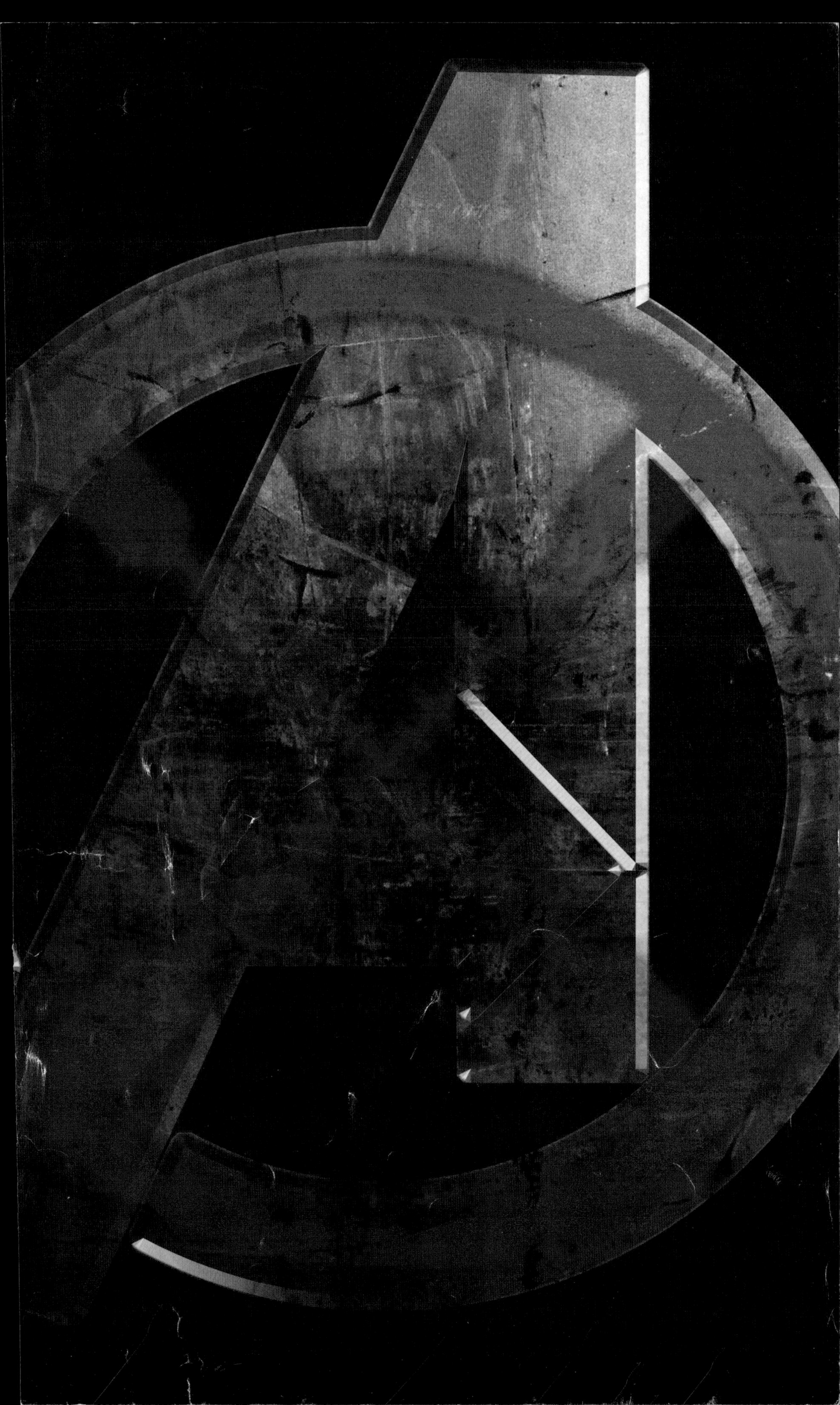

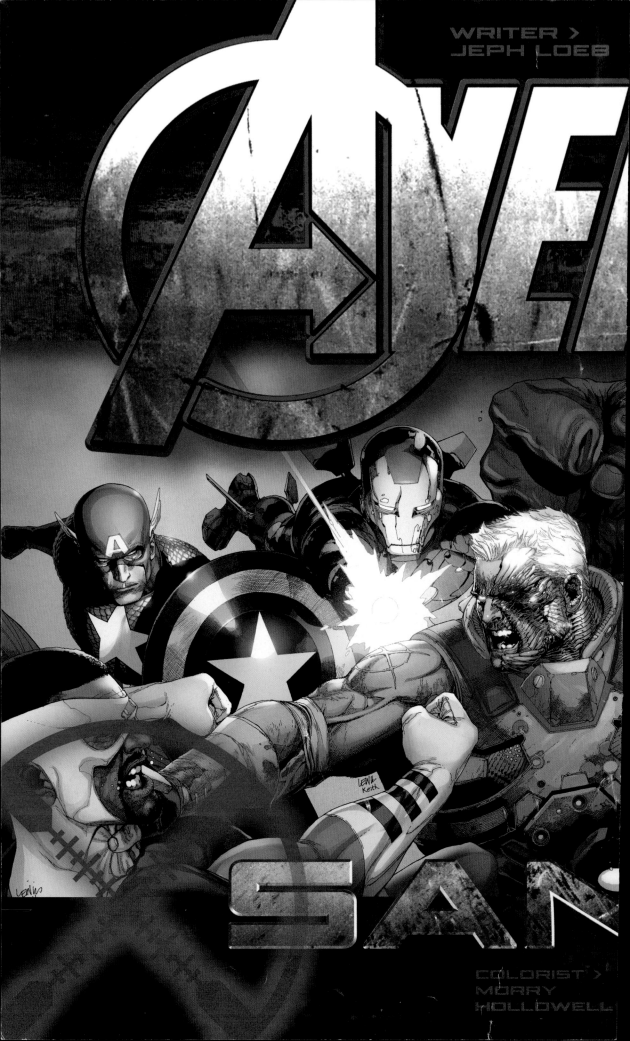

WRITER >
JEPH LOEB

COLORIST >
MORRY
HOLLOWELL

PENCILER >
ED McGUINNESS

INKER >
DEXTER VINES

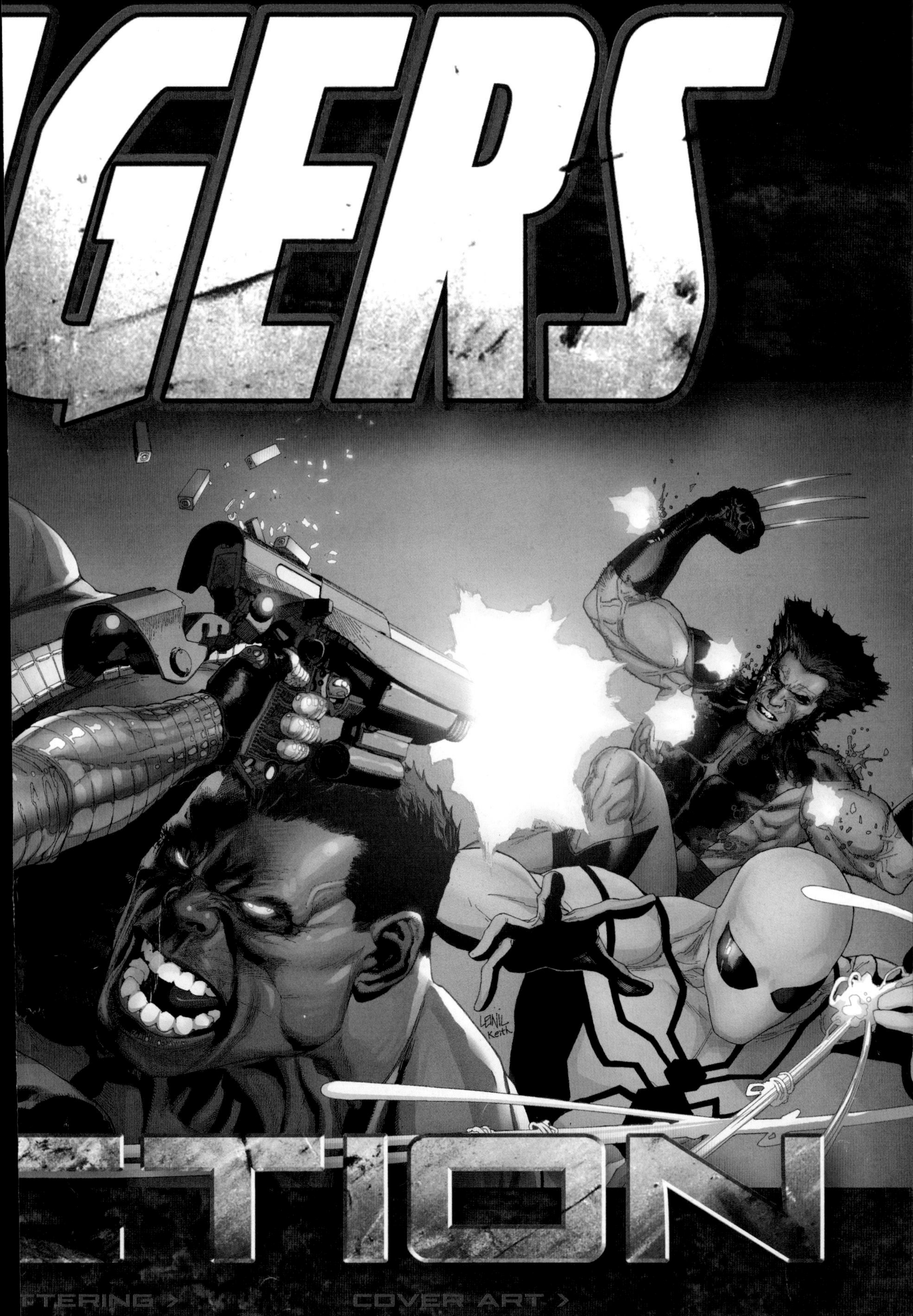
GERS
TION

TTERING >
MICRAFT'S
BER DESCHESNE

COVER ART >
ED McGUINNESS, DEXTER
VINES & MORRY HOLLOWELL

ASSISTANT EDITOR > JOHN DENNING
ASSOCIATE EDITOR > LAUREN SANKOVITCH
EDITOR > TOM BREVOORT

COLLECTION EDITOR > JENNIFER GRÜNWALD
ASSISTANT EDITORS > ALEX STARBUCK & NELSON RIBEIRO
EDITOR, SPECIAL PROJECTS > MARK D. BEAZLEY
SENIOR EDITOR, SPECIAL PROJECTS > JEFF YOUNGQUIST
SENIOR VICE PRESIDENT OF SALES > DAVID GABRIEL
SVP OF BRAND PLANNING & COMMUNICATIONS > MICHAEL PASCIULLO
BOOK DESIGNER > JOHN ROSHELL OF COMICRAFT

EDITOR IN CHIEF > AXEL ALONSO
CHIEF CREATIVE OFFICER > JOE QUESADA
PUBLISHER > DAN BUCKLEY
EXECUTIVE PRODUCER > ALAN FINE

AVENGERS: X-SANCTION. Contains material originally published in magazine form as AVENGERS: X-SANCTION #1-4. First printing 2012. ISBN# 978-0-7851-5862-2. Published by MARVEL WORLDWIDE, INC., a subsidiary of MARVEL ENTERTAINMENT, LLC. OFFICE OF PUBLICATION: 135 West 50th Street, New York, NY 10020. $24.99 per copy in the U.S. and $27.99 in Canada (GST #R127032852); Canadian Agreement #40668537. Printed in the U.S.A. ALAN FINE, EVP - Office of the President, Marvel Worldwide, Inc. and EVP & CMO Marvel Characters B.V.; DAN BUCKLEY, Publisher & President - Print, Animation & Digital Divisions; JOE QUESADA, Chief Creative Officer; TOM BREVOORT, SVP of Publishing; DAVID BOGART, SVP of Operations & Procurement, Publishing; RUWAN JAYATILLEKE, SVP & Associate Publisher, Publishing; C.B. CEBULSKI, SVP of Creator & Content Development; DAVID GABRIEL, SVP of Publishing Sales & Circulation; MICHAEL PASCIULLO, SVP of Brand Planning & Communications; JIM O'KEEFE, VP of Operations & Logistics; DAN CARR, Executive Director of Publishing Technology; SUSAN CRESPI, Editorial Operations Manager; ALEX MORALES, Publishing Operations Manager; STAN LEE, Chairman Emeritus. For information regarding advertising in Marvel Comics or on Marvel.com, please contact John Dokes, SVP Integrated Sales and Marketing, at jdokes@marvel.com. For Marvel subscription inquiries, please call 800-217-9158. Manufactured between 3/19/2012 and 4/16/2012 by R.R. DONNELLEY, INC., SALEM, VA, USA.

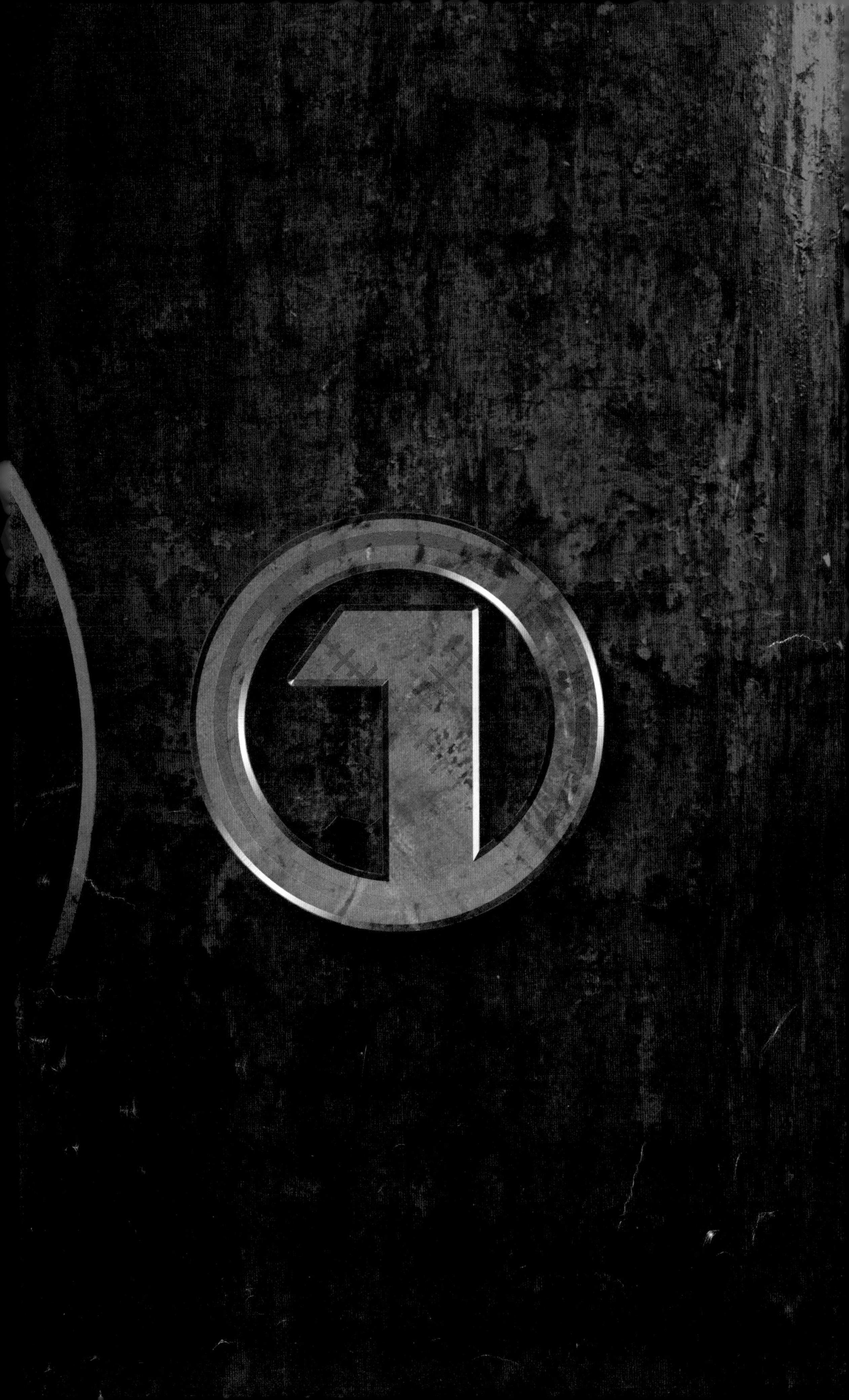
1

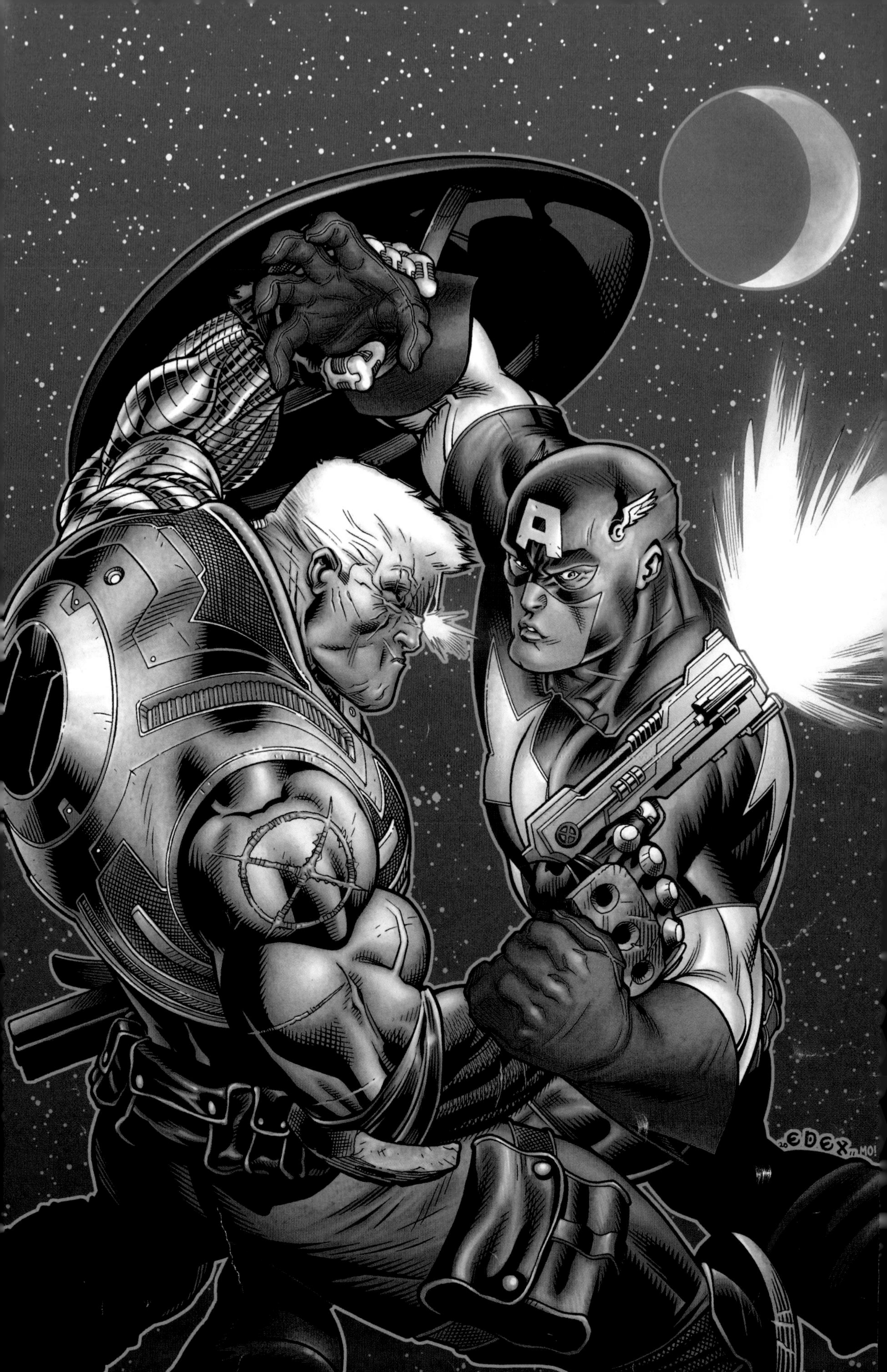

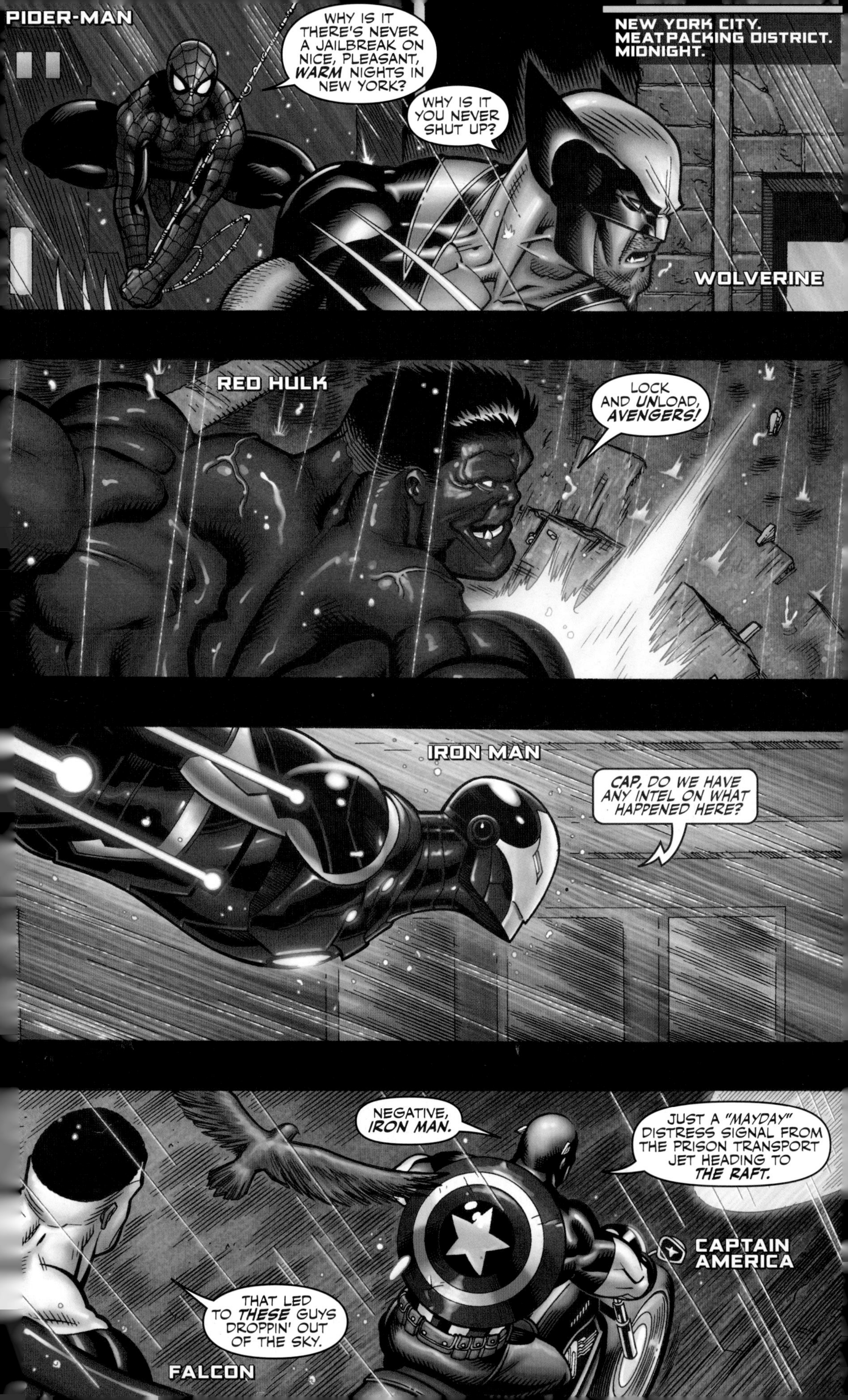
PIDER-MAN
WHY IS IT THERE'S NEVER A JAILBREAK ON NICE, PLEASANT, WARM NIGHTS IN NEW YORK?
NEW YORK CITY. MEATPACKING DISTRICT. MIDNIGHT.
WHY IS IT YOU NEVER SHUT UP?
WOLVERINE
RED HULK
LOCK AND UNLOAD, AVENGERS!
IRON MAN
CAP, DO WE HAVE ANY INTEL ON WHAT HAPPENED HERE?
NEGATIVE, IRON MAN.
JUST A "MAYDAY" DISTRESS SIGNAL FROM THE PRISON TRANSPORT JET HEADING TO THE RAFT.
CAPTAIN AMERICA
THAT LED TO THESE GUYS DROPPIN' OUT OF THE SKY.
FALCON

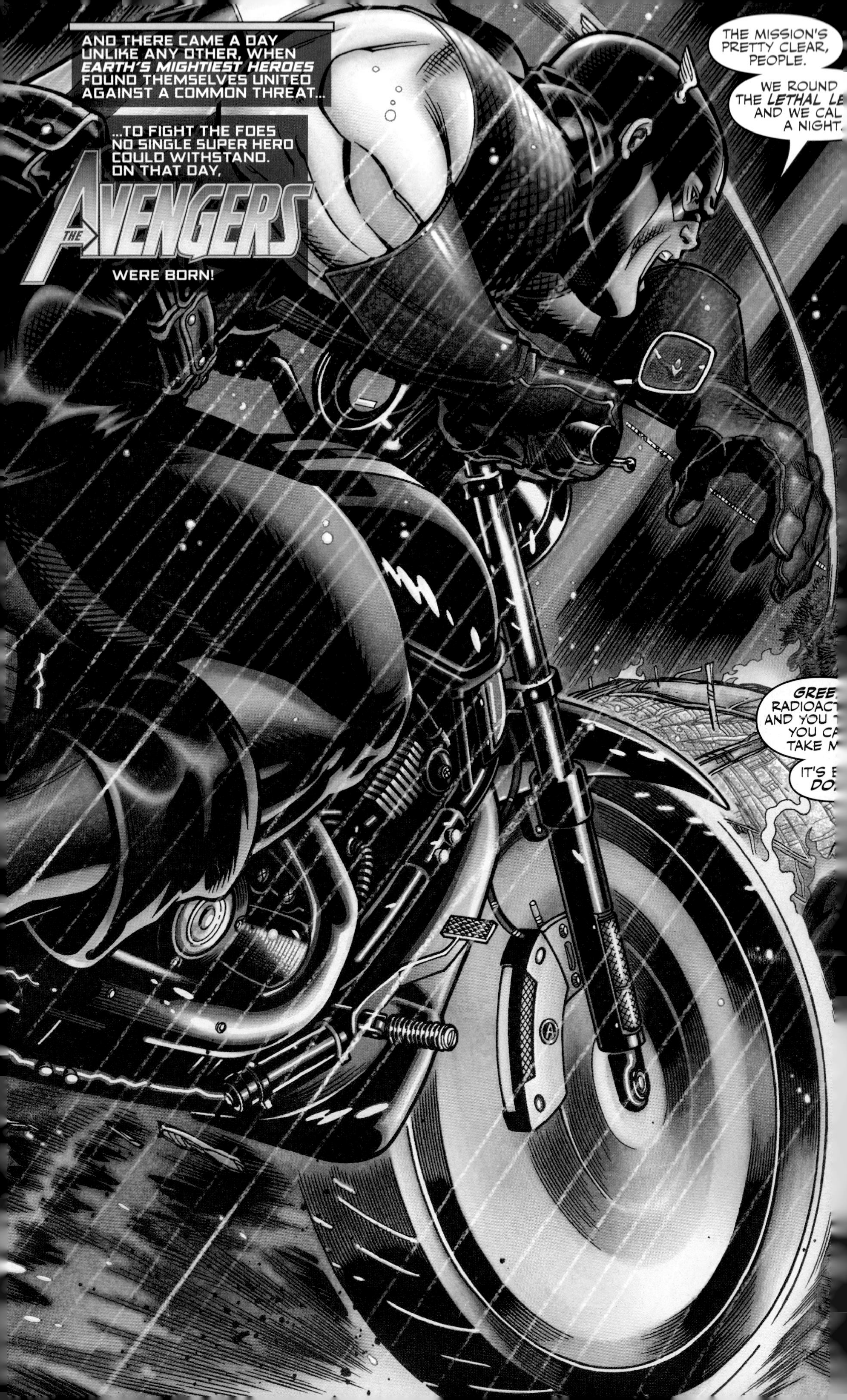

AND THERE CAME A DAY UNLIKE ANY OTHER, WHEN *EARTH'S MIGHTIEST HEROES* FOUND THEMSELVES UNITED AGAINST A COMMON THREAT...
...TO FIGHT THE FOES NO SINGLE SUPER HERO COULD WITHSTAND. ON THAT DAY,
THE AVENGERS
WERE BORN!
THE MISSION'S PRETTY CLEAR, PEOPLE.
WE ROUND THE *LETHAL LE* AND WE CAL A NIGHT.

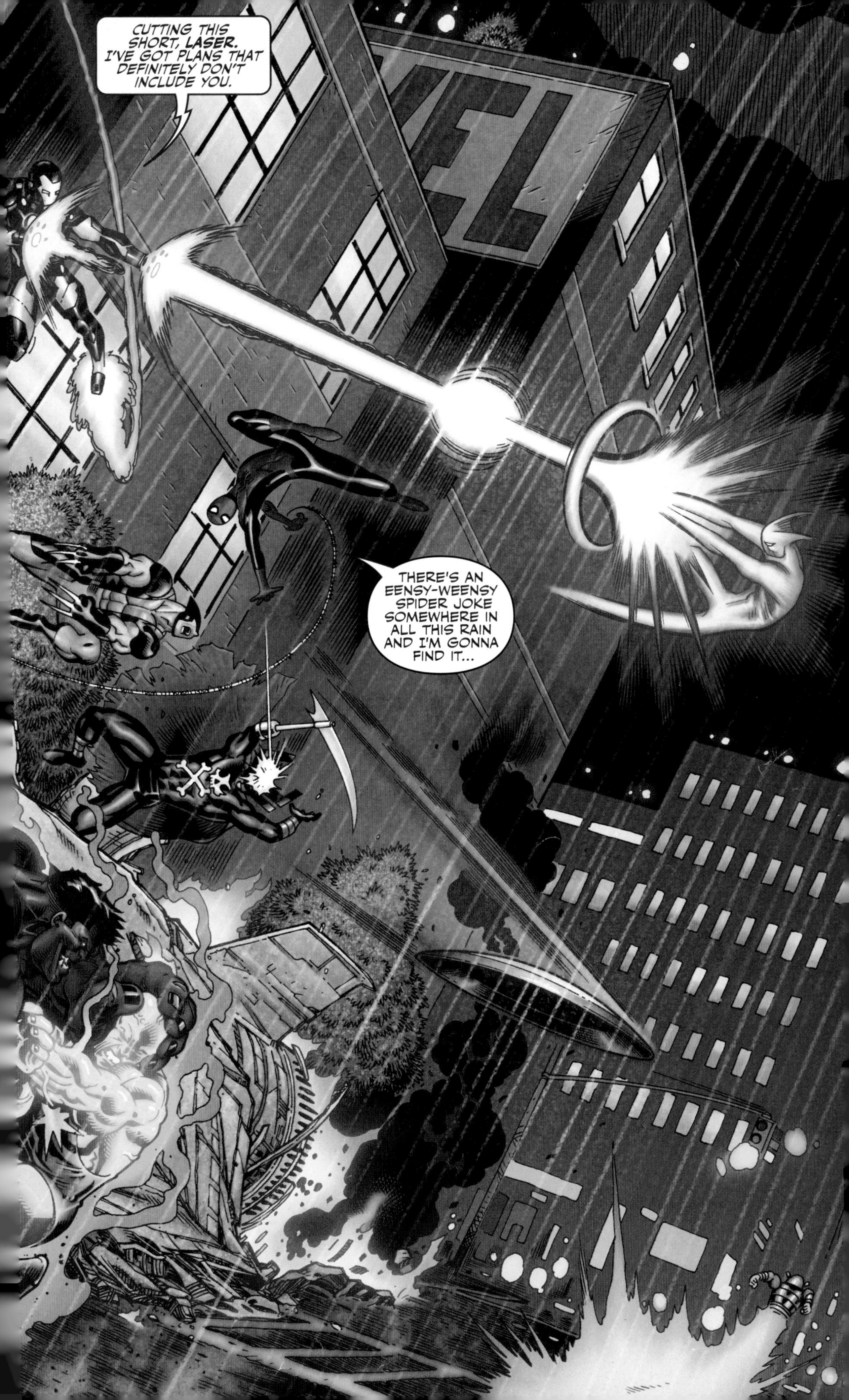
CUTTING THIS SHORT, LASER. I'VE GOT PLANS THAT DEFINITELY DON'T INCLUDE YOU.
THERE'S AN EENSY-WEENSY SPIDER JOKE SOMEWHERE IN ALL THIS RAIN AND I'M GONNA FIND IT...

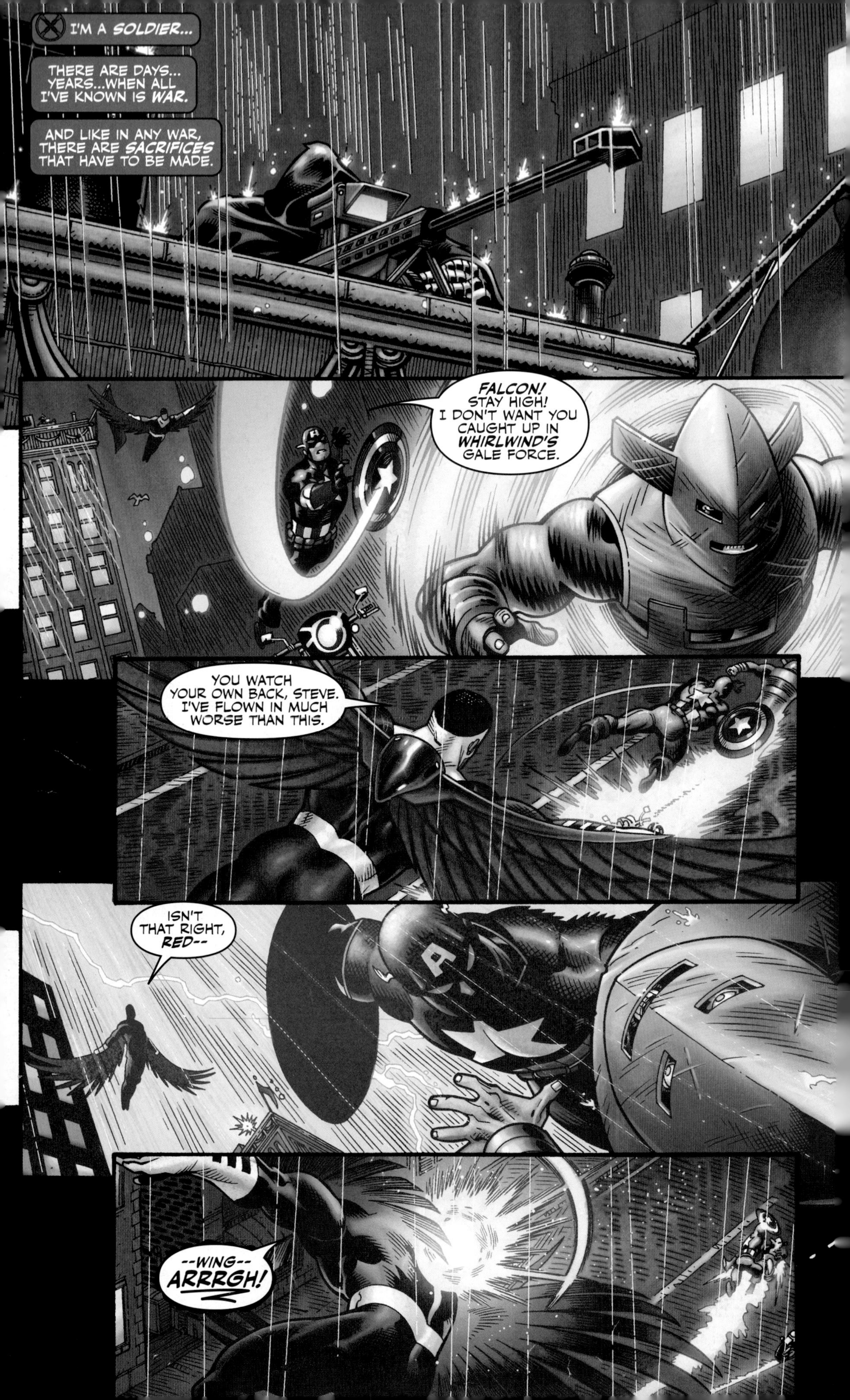
I'M A SOLDIER...
THERE ARE DAYS... YEARS...WHEN ALL I'VE KNOWN IS WAR.
AND LIKE IN ANY WAR, THERE ARE SACRIFICES THAT HAVE TO BE MADE.
FALCON! STAY HIGH! I DON'T WANT YOU CAUGHT UP IN WHIRLWIND'S GALE FORCE.
YOU WATCH YOUR OWN BACK, STEVE. I'VE FLOWN IN MUCH WORSE THAN THIS.
ISN'T THAT RIGHT, RED--
--WING--
ARRRGH!

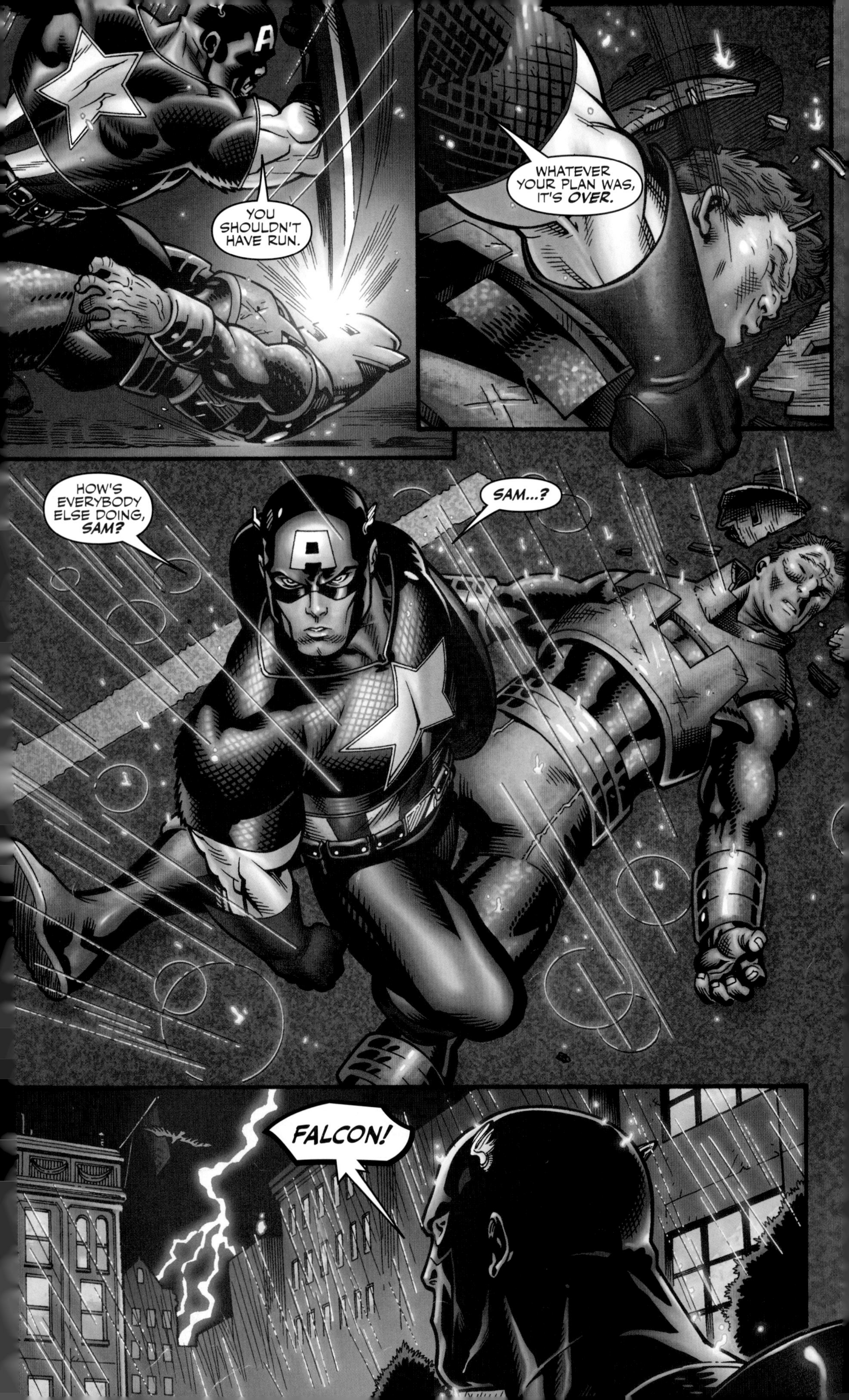
YOU SHOULDN'T HAVE RUN.
WHATEVER YOUR PLAN WAS, IT'S OVER.
HOW'S EVERYBODY ELSE DOING, SAM?
SAM...?
FALCON!

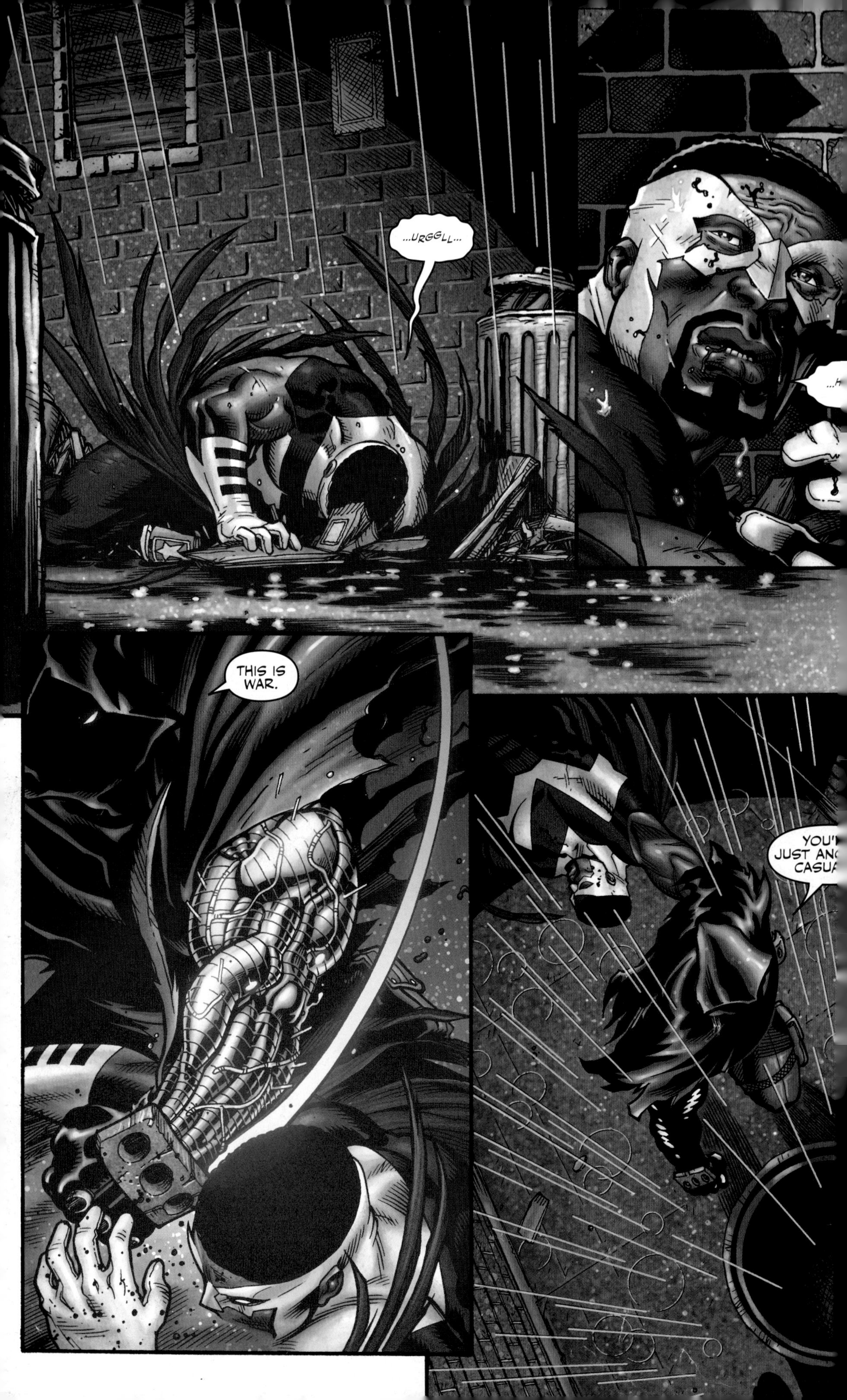
...URGGLL...
THIS IS WAR.
YOU' JUST AN CASUA

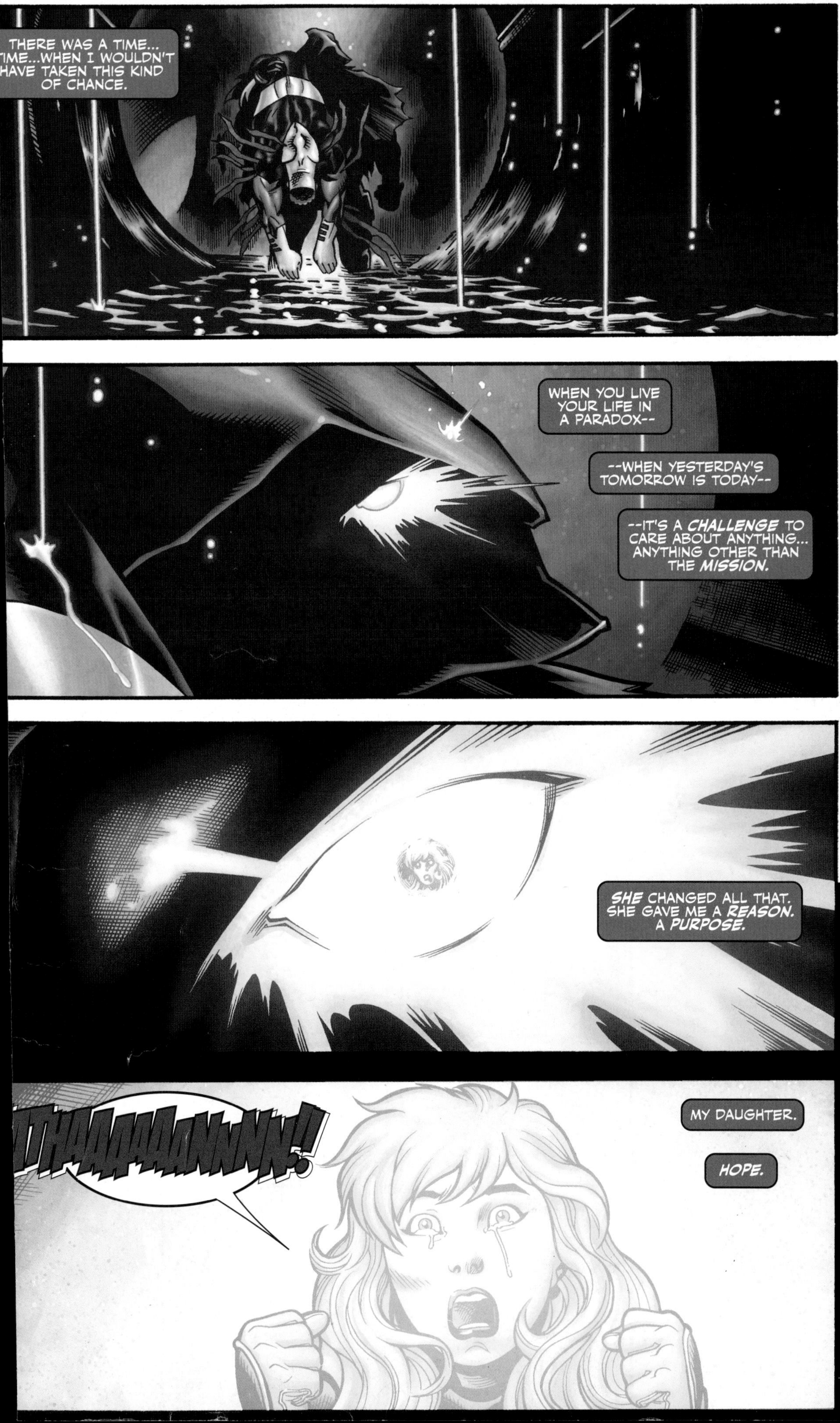
THERE WAS A TIME... TIME...WHEN I WOULDN'T HAVE TAKEN THIS KIND OF CHANCE.
WHEN YOU LIVE YOUR LIFE IN A PARADOX--
--WHEN YESTERDAY'S TOMORROW IS TODAY--
--IT'S A CHALLENGE TO CARE ABOUT ANYTHING... ANYTHING OTHER THAN THE MISSION.
SHE CHANGED ALL THAT. SHE GAVE ME A REASON. A PURPOSE.
MY DAUGHTER.
HOPE.

IMAGINE.

THE LAST FACE YOU EVER SEE...

...IS YOUR CHILD WATCHING YOU DIE...

TIMESLIDE. THE FAR FUTURE.

HELLO...?!

IS ANYBODY OUT THERE?!

HELLLLLLOOOO!

OH...

...HELL..

IT WAS A TIME...T[...] THE HEAT...OPPRES[...]

...NOTHING... BUT ASH...

...MAYBE I DID DIE...

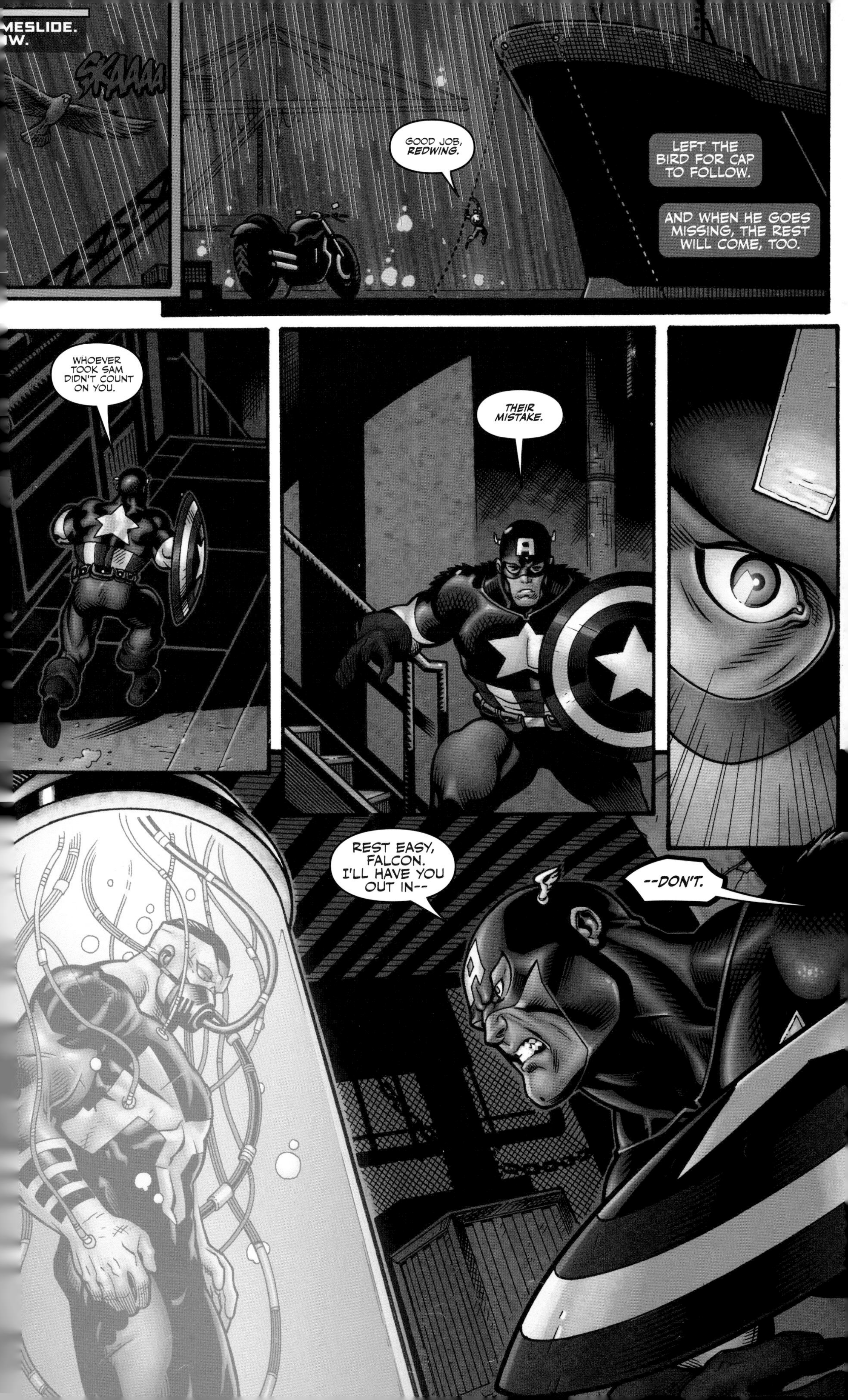
MESLIDE.
W.
SKAAAA
GOOD JOB, REDWING.
LEFT THE BIRD FOR CAP TO FOLLOW.
AND WHEN HE GOES MISSING, THE REST WILL COME, TOO.
WHOEVER TOOK SAM DIDN'T COUNT ON YOU.
THEIR MISTAKE.
REST EASY, FALCON. I'LL HAVE YOU OUT IN--
--DON'T.

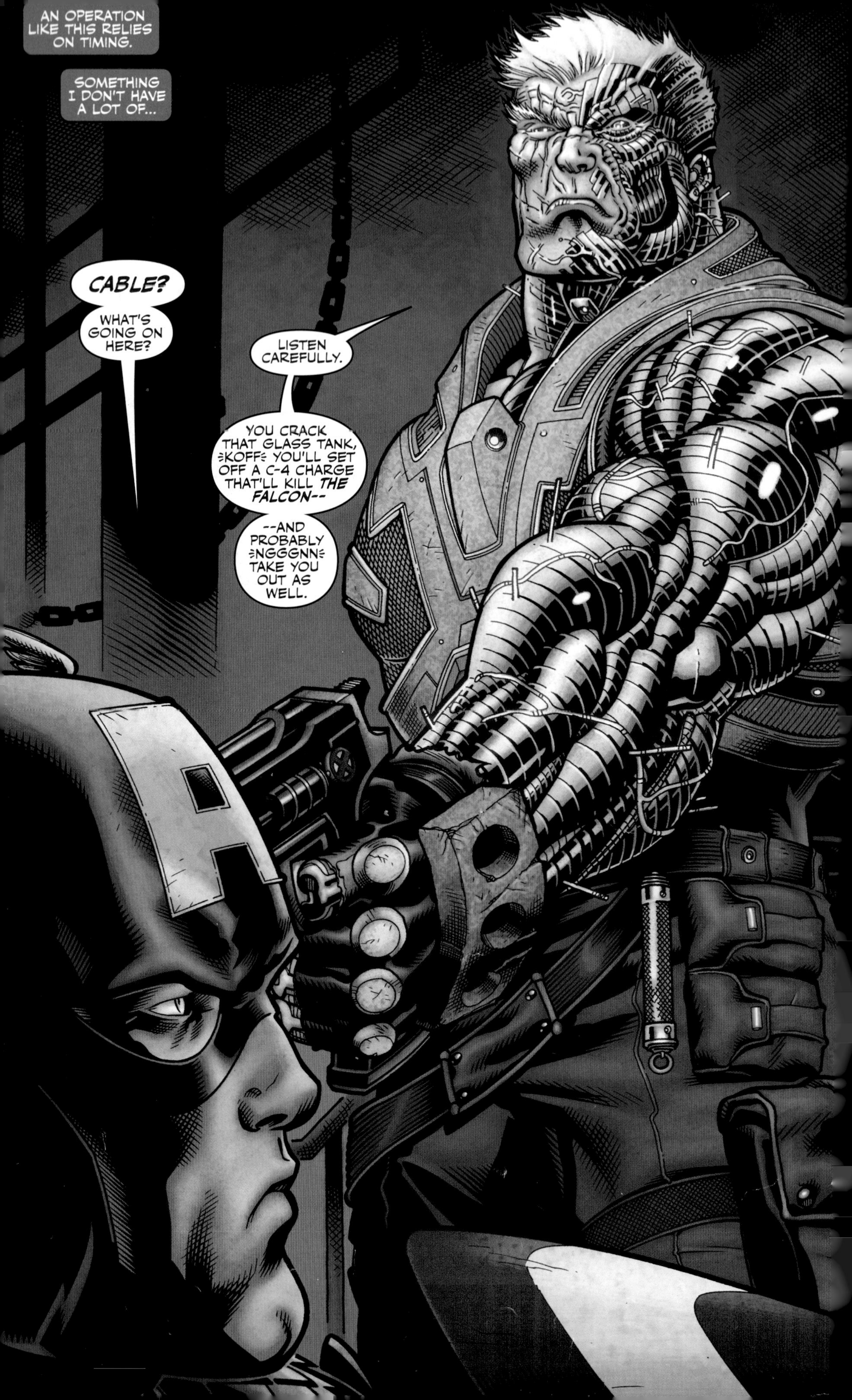
AN OPERATION LIKE THIS RELIES ON TIMING.
SOMETHING I DON'T HAVE A LOT OF...
CABLE?
WHAT'S GOING ON HERE?
LISTEN CAREFULLY.
YOU CRACK THAT GLASS TANK, =KOFF= YOU'LL SET OFF A C-4 CHARGE THAT'LL KILL THE FALCON--
--AND PROBABLY =NGGGNN= TAKE YOU OUT AS WELL.

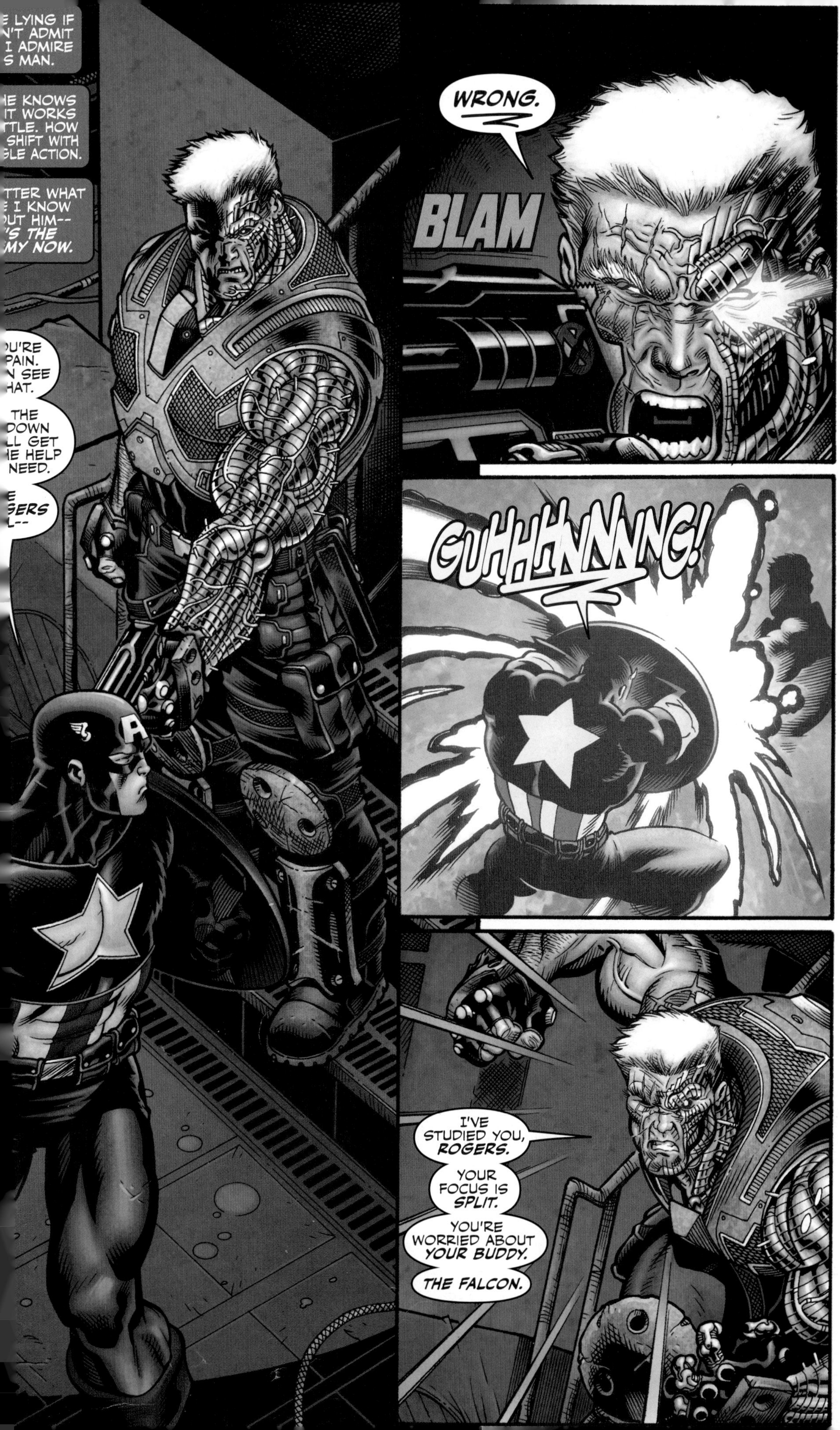

E LYING IF N'T ADMIT I ADMIRE S MAN.
HE KNOWS IT WORKS TTLE. HOW SHIFT WITH GLE ACTION.
TTER WHAT E I KNOW UT HIM-- 'S THE MY NOW.
U'RE PAIN. N SEE HAT.
THE DOWN LL GET E HELP NEED.
E GERS L--
WRONG.
BLAM
GUHHHNNNNG!
I'VE STUDIED YOU, ROGERS.
YOUR FOCUS IS SPLIT.
YOU'RE WORRIED ABOUT YOUR BUDDY.
THE FALCON.

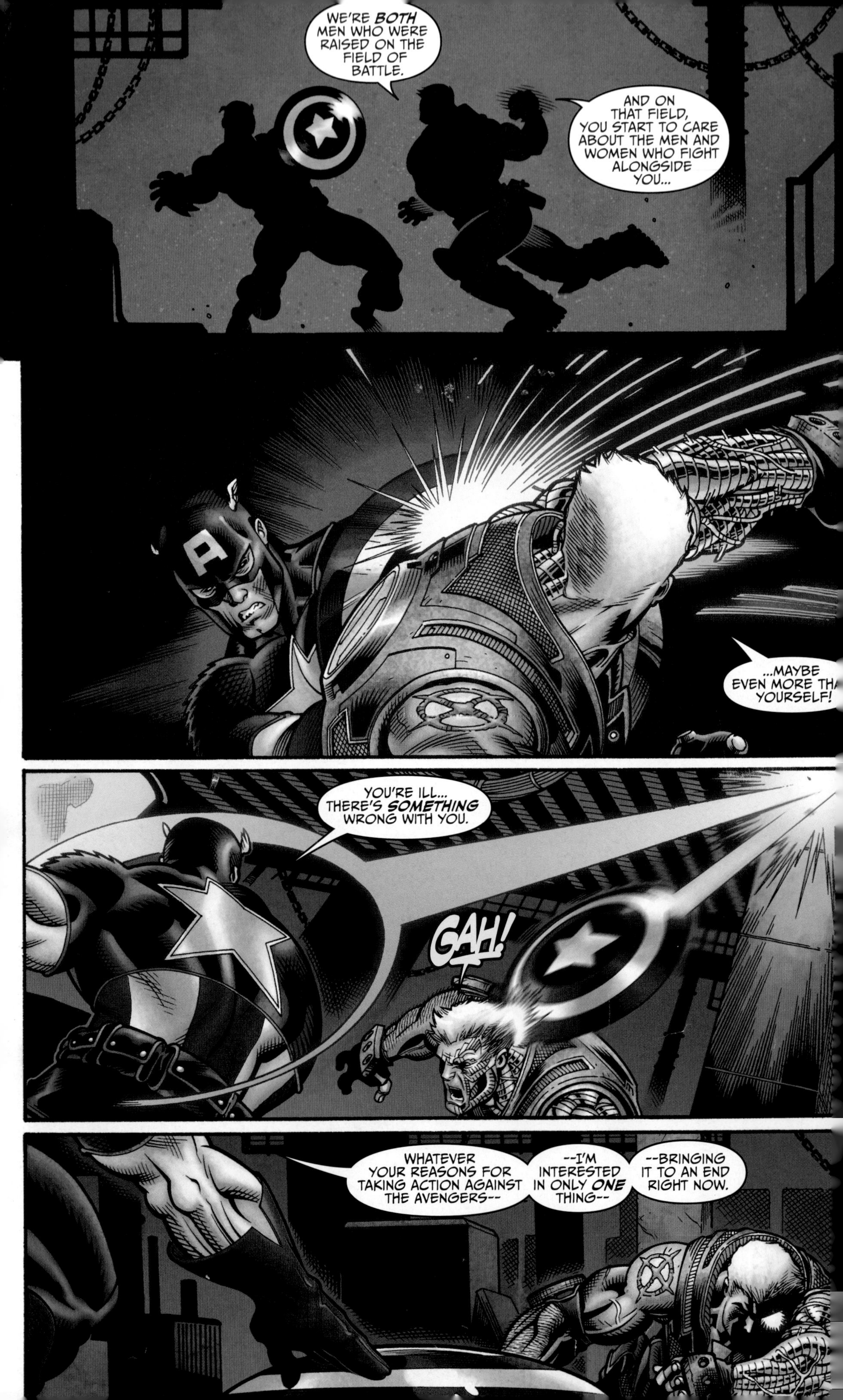
WE'RE BOTH MEN WHO WERE RAISED ON THE FIELD OF BATTLE.
AND ON THAT FIELD, YOU START TO CARE ABOUT THE MEN AND WOMEN WHO FIGHT ALONGSIDE YOU...
...MAYBE EVEN MORE THA YOURSELF!
YOU'RE ILL... THERE'S SOMETHING WRONG WITH YOU.
GAH!
WHATEVER YOUR REASONS FOR TAKING ACTION AGAINST THE AVENGERS--
--I'M INTERESTED IN ONLY ONE THING--
--BRINGING IT TO AN END RIGHT NOW.

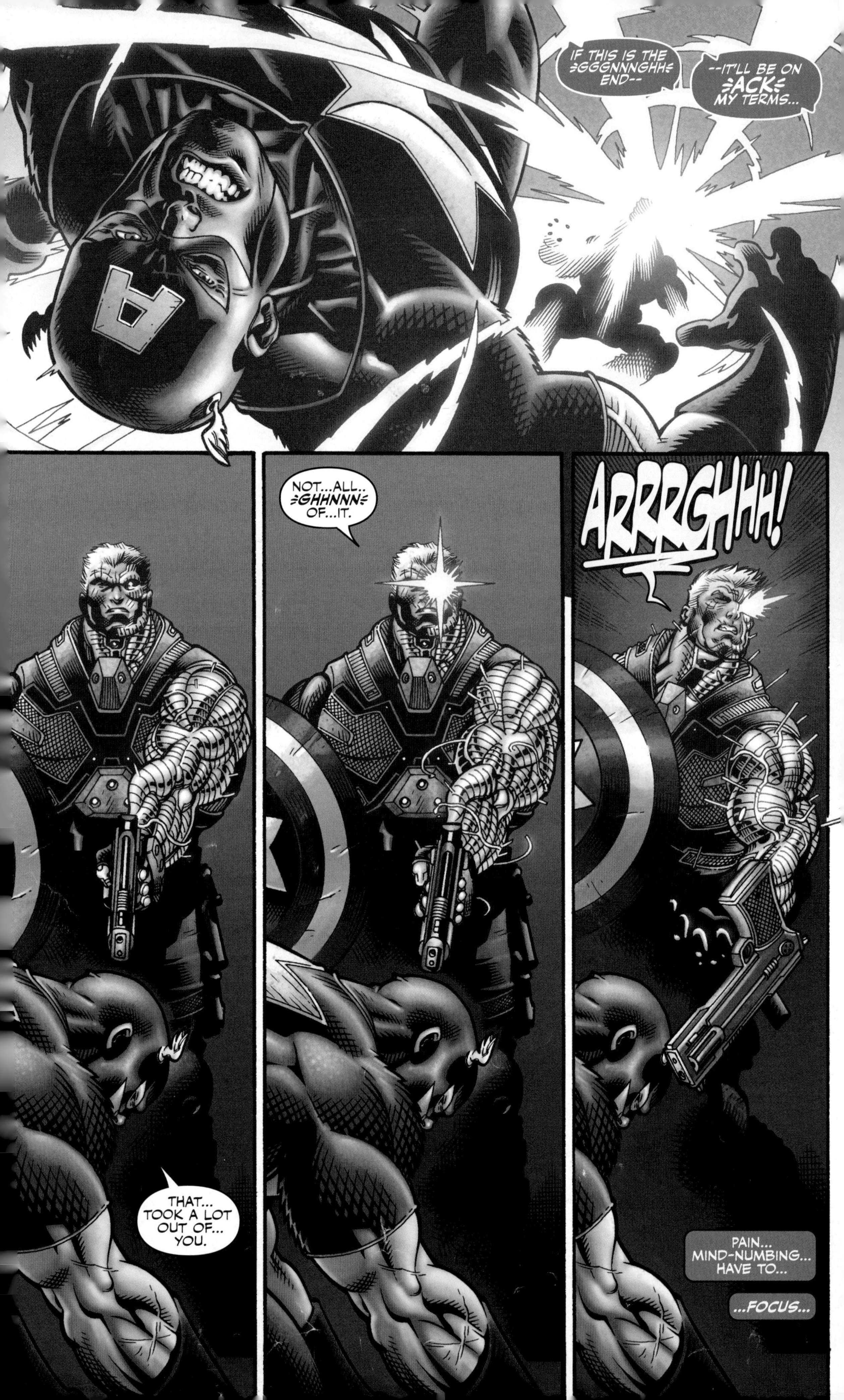
IF THIS IS THE
GGGNNNGHH
END--
--IT'LL BE ON
ACK
MY TERMS...
THAT... TOOK A LOT OUT OF... YOU.
NOT...ALL.. GHHNNN OF...IT.
ARRRGHHH!
PAIN... MIND-NUMBING... HAVE TO...
...FOCUS...

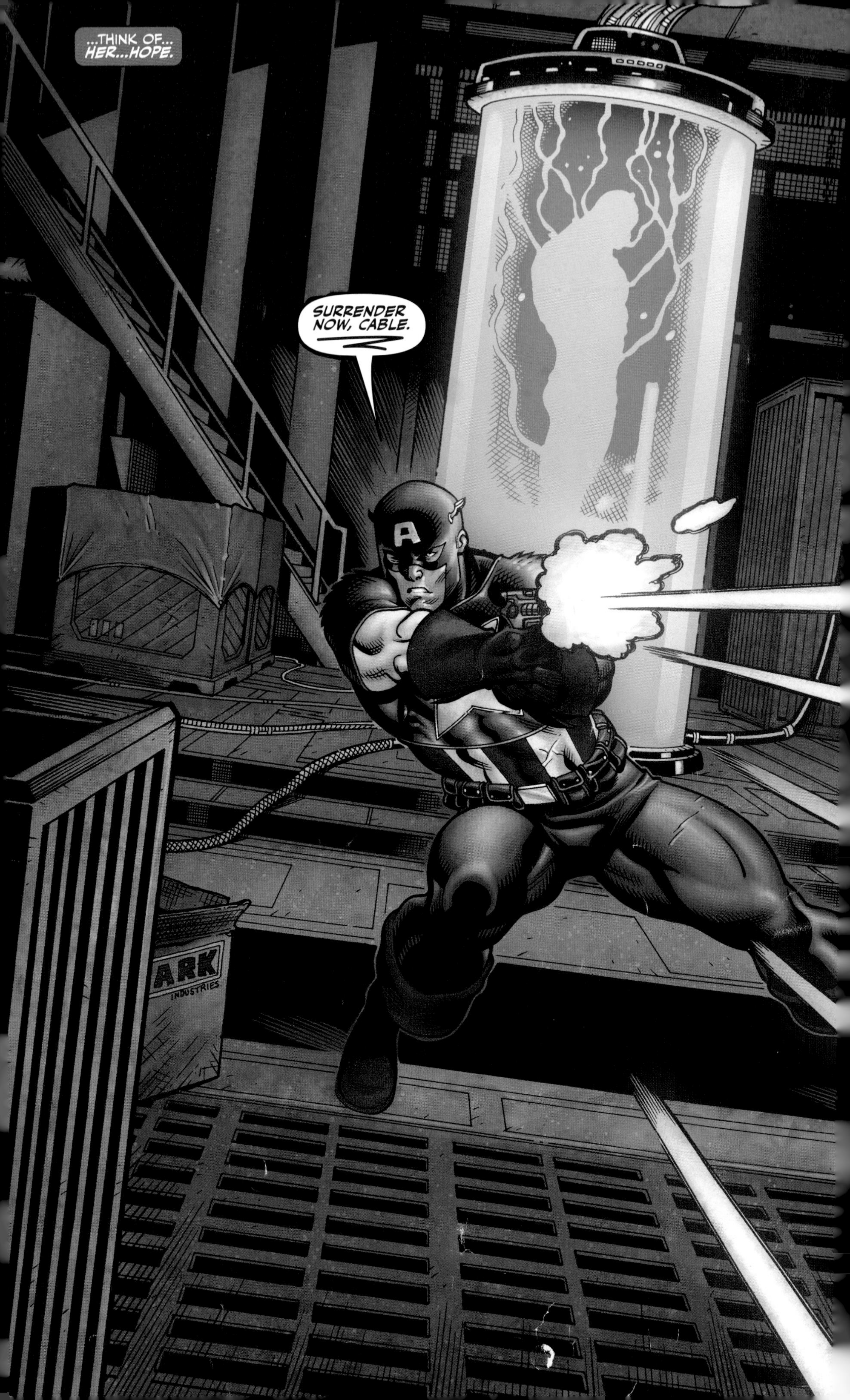
...THINK OF...
HER...HOPE.
SURRENDER NOW, CABLE.
ARK
INDUSTRIES

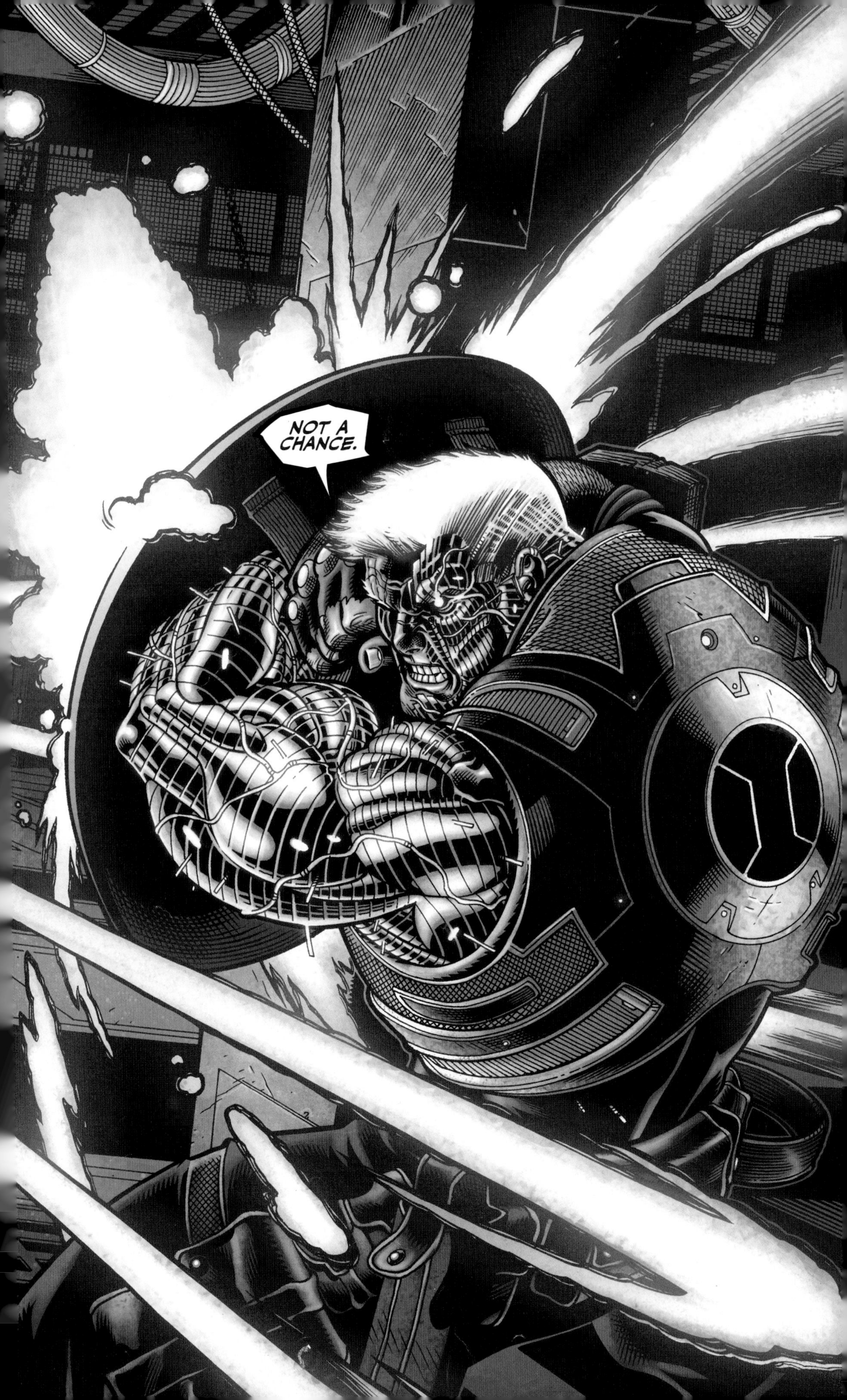
NOT A CHANCE.

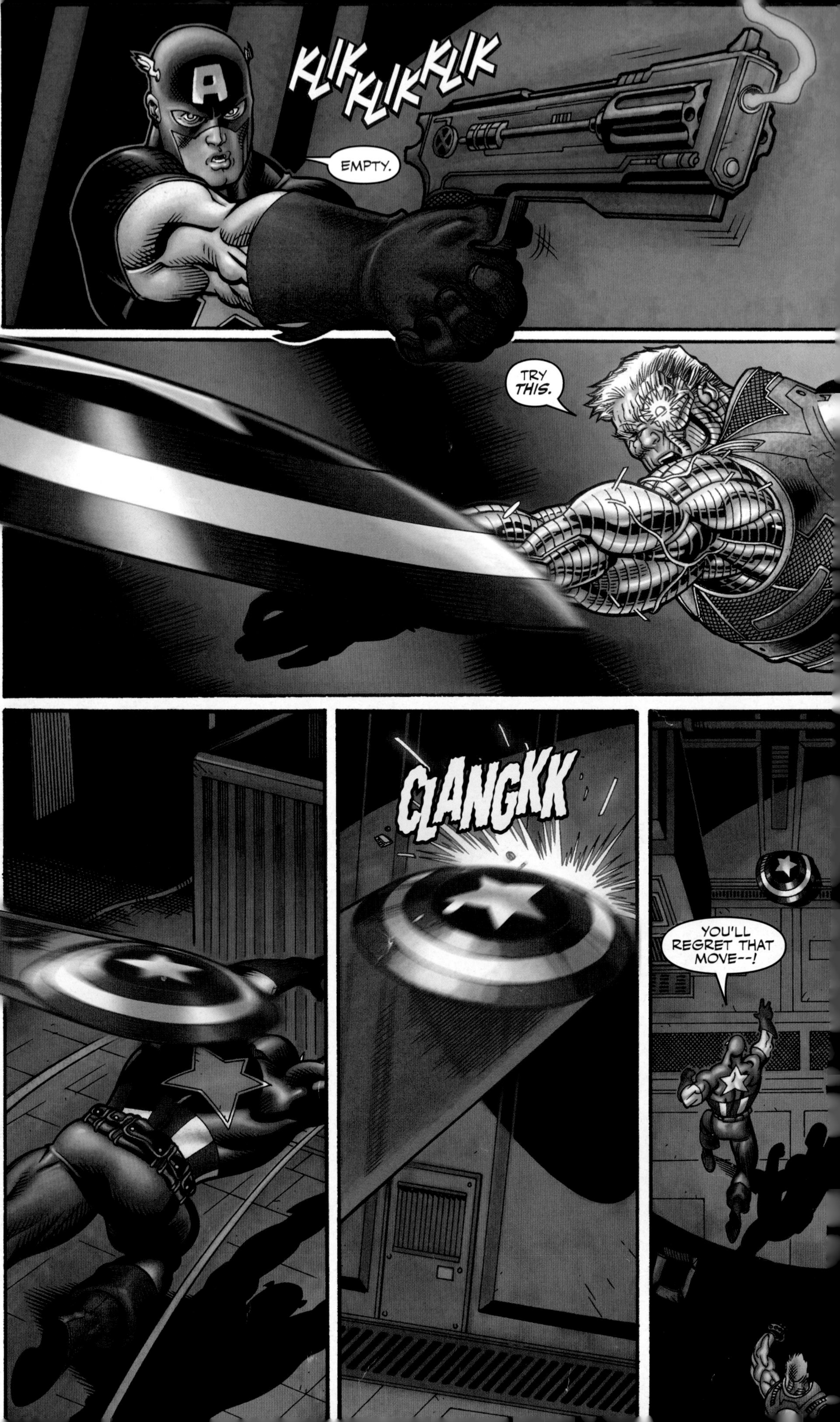
KLIK KLIK KLIK
EMPTY.
TRY THIS.
CLANGKK
YOU'LL REGRET THAT MOVE--!

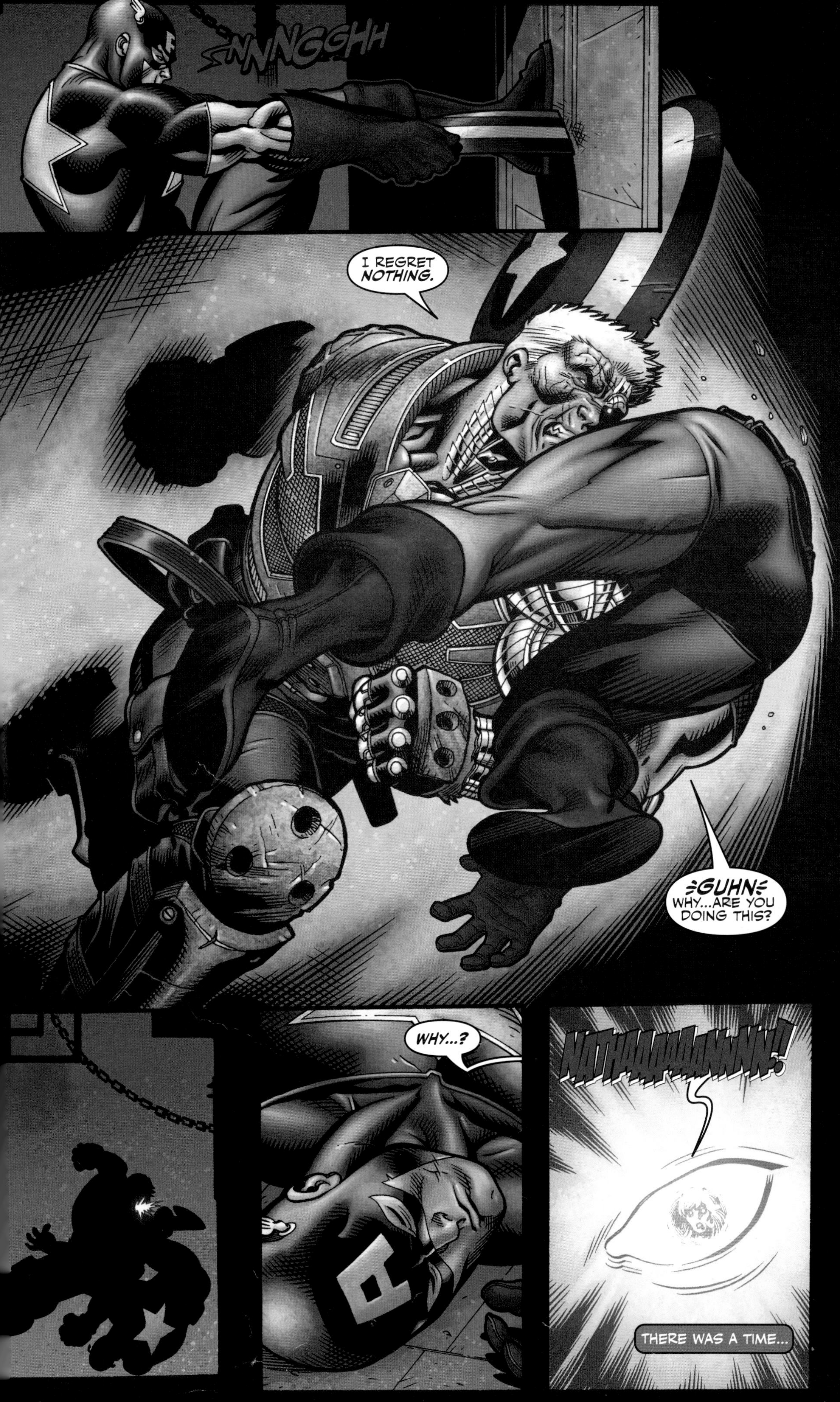
SNNNGGHH
I REGRET NOTHING.
GUHN
WHY...ARE YOU DOING THIS?
WHY...?
NATHAAAAAANNNN!!
THERE WAS A TIME...

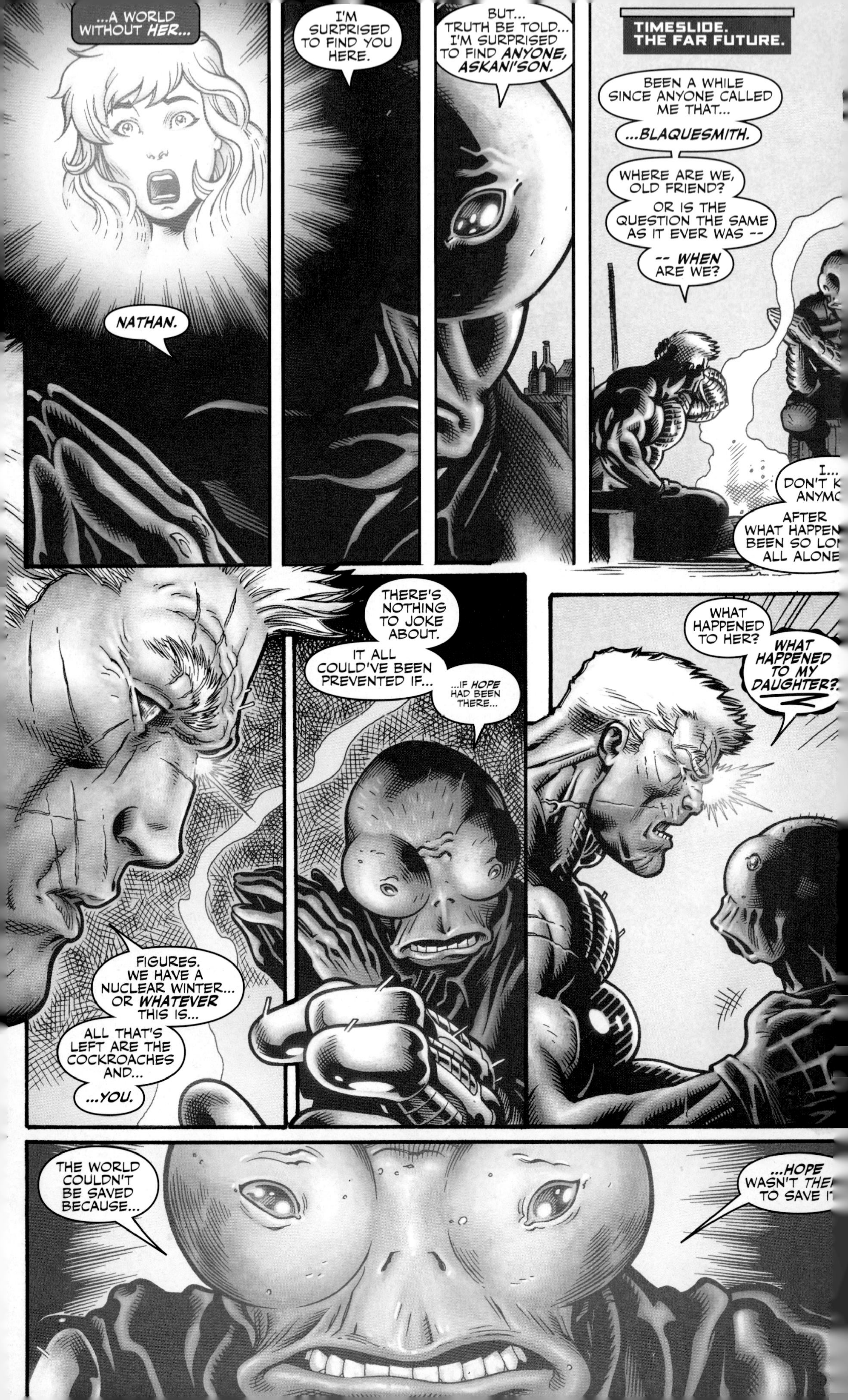
...A WORLD WITHOUT HER...
NATHAN.
I'M SURPRISED TO FIND YOU HERE.
BUT... TRUTH BE TOLD... I'M SURPRISED TO FIND ANYONE, ASKANI'SON.
TIMESLIDE. THE FAR FUTURE.
BEEN A WHILE SINCE ANYONE CALLED ME THAT...
...BLAQUESMITH.
WHERE ARE WE, OLD FRIEND?
OR IS THE QUESTION THE SAME AS IT EVER WAS --
-- WHEN ARE WE?
I... DON'T K ANYMO
AFTER WHAT HAPPEN BEEN SO LO ALL ALONE
FIGURES. WE HAVE A NUCLEAR WINTER... OR WHATEVER THIS IS...
ALL THAT'S LEFT ARE THE COCKROACHES AND...
...YOU.
THERE'S NOTHING TO JOKE ABOUT.
IT ALL COULD'VE BEEN PREVENTED IF...
...IF HOPE HAD BEEN THERE...
WHAT HAPPENED TO HER?
WHAT HAPPENED TO MY DAUGHTER?
THE WORLD COULDN'T BE SAVED BECAUSE...
...HOPE WASN'T THE TO SAVE I

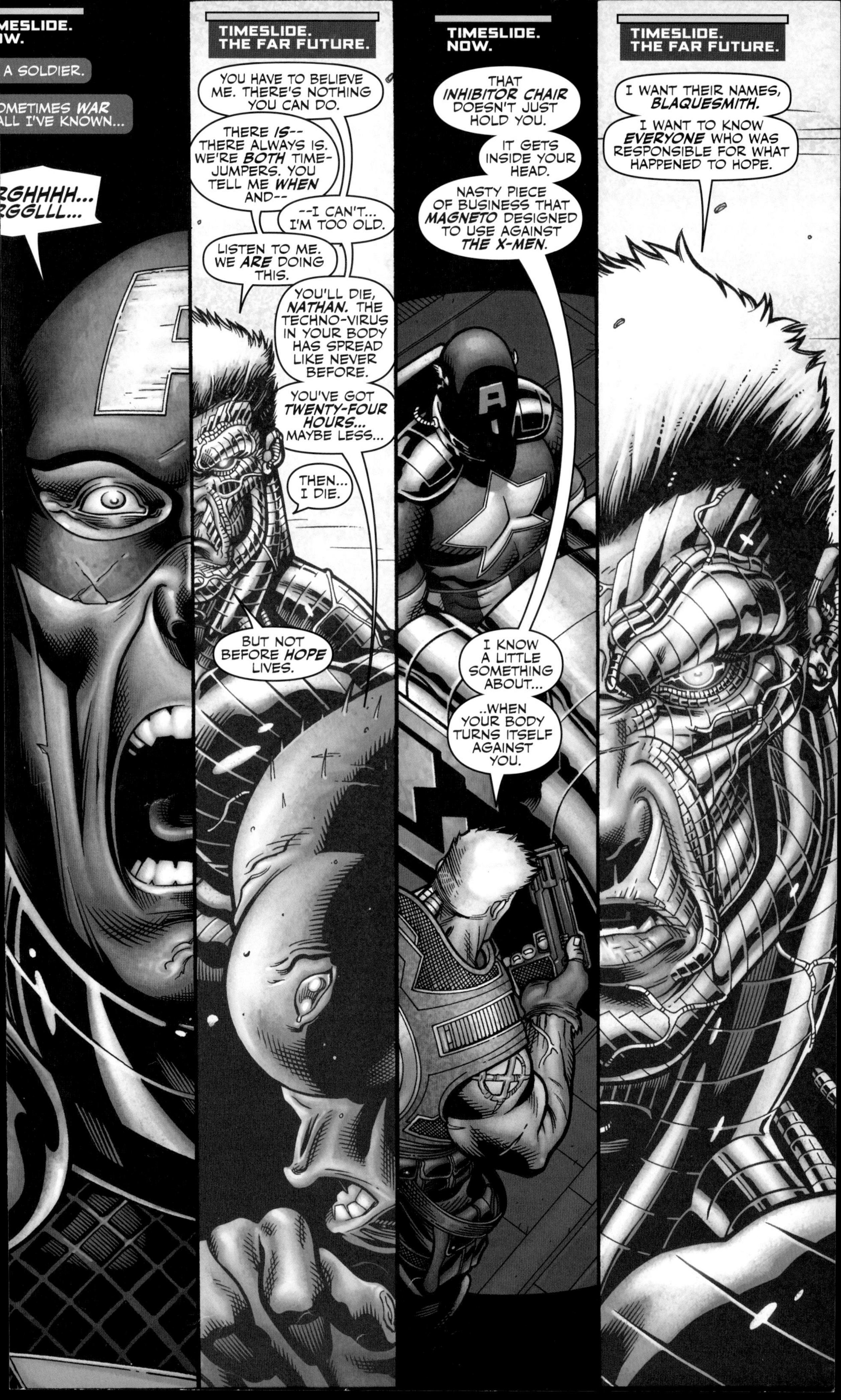

IMESLIDE.
W.
A SOLDIER.
OMETIMES WAR
ALL I'VE KNOWN...
RGHHHH...
RGGLLL...
TIMESLIDE. THE FAR FUTURE.
YOU HAVE TO BELIEVE ME. THERE'S NOTHING YOU CAN DO.
THERE IS-- THERE ALWAYS IS. WE'RE BOTH TIME-JUMPERS. YOU TELL ME WHEN AND--
--I CAN'T... I'M TOO OLD.
LISTEN TO ME. WE ARE DOING THIS.
YOU'LL DIE, NATHAN. THE TECHNO-VIRUS IN YOUR BODY HAS SPREAD LIKE NEVER BEFORE.
YOU'VE GOT TWENTY-FOUR HOURS... MAYBE LESS...
THEN... I DIE.
BUT NOT BEFORE HOPE LIVES.
TIMESLIDE. NOW.
THAT INHIBITOR CHAIR DOESN'T JUST HOLD YOU.
IT GETS INSIDE YOUR HEAD.
NASTY PIECE OF BUSINESS THAT MAGNETO DESIGNED TO USE AGAINST THE X-MEN.
I KNOW A LITTLE SOMETHING ABOUT...
..WHEN YOUR BODY TURNS ITSELF AGAINST YOU.
TIMESLIDE. THE FAR FUTURE.
I WANT THEIR NAMES, BLAQUESMITH.
I WANT TO KNOW EVERYONE WHO WAS RESPONSIBLE FOR WHAT HAPPENED TO HOPE.

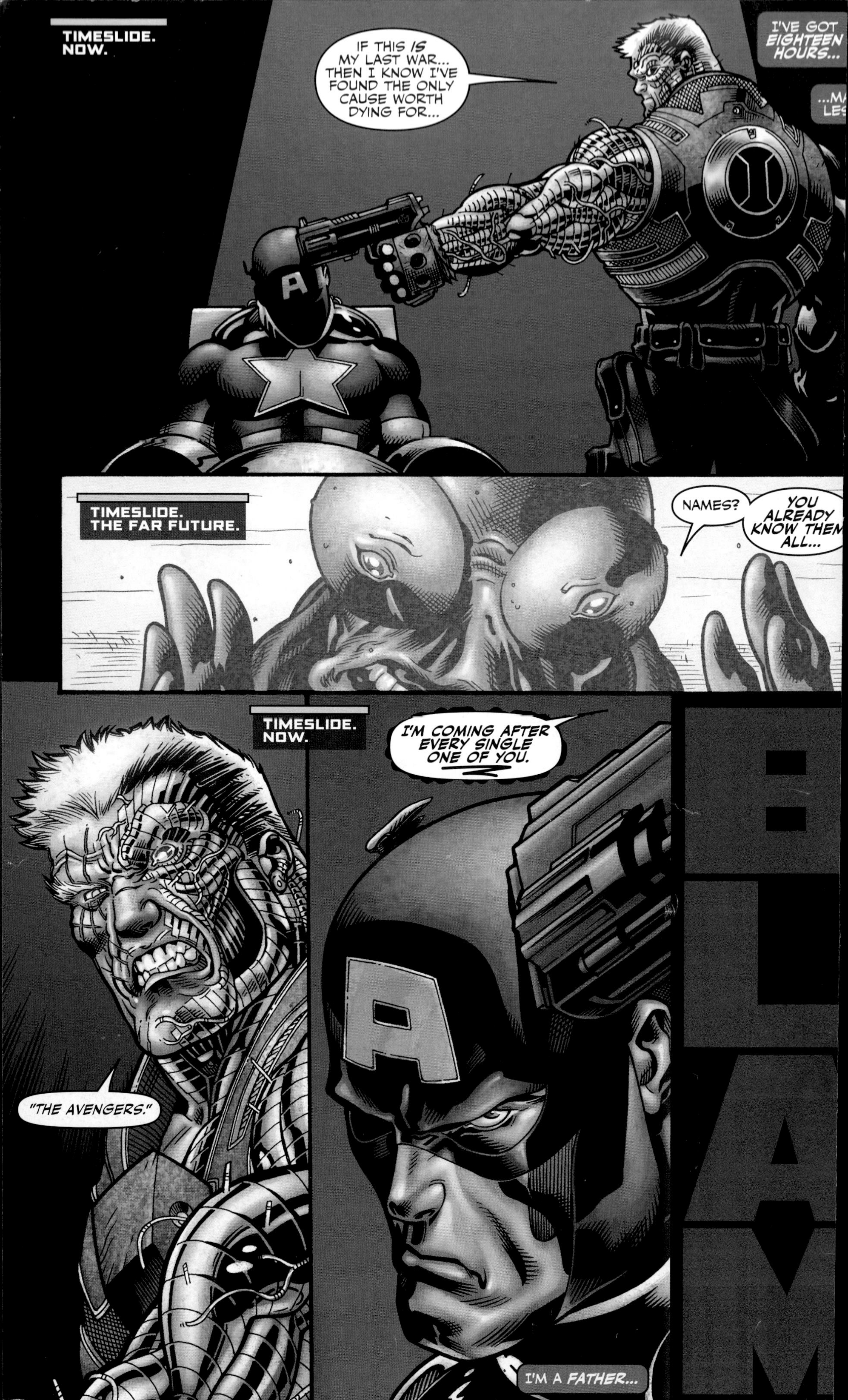
TIMESLIDE. NOW.
IF THIS IS MY LAST WAR... THEN I KNOW I'VE FOUND THE ONLY CAUSE WORTH DYING FOR...
I'VE GOT EIGHTEEN HOURS...
TIMESLIDE. THE FAR FUTURE.
NAMES?
YOU ALREADY KNOW THEM ALL...
TIMESLIDE. NOW.
"THE AVENGERS."
I'M COMING AFTER EVERY SINGLE ONE OF YOU.
I'M A FATHER...

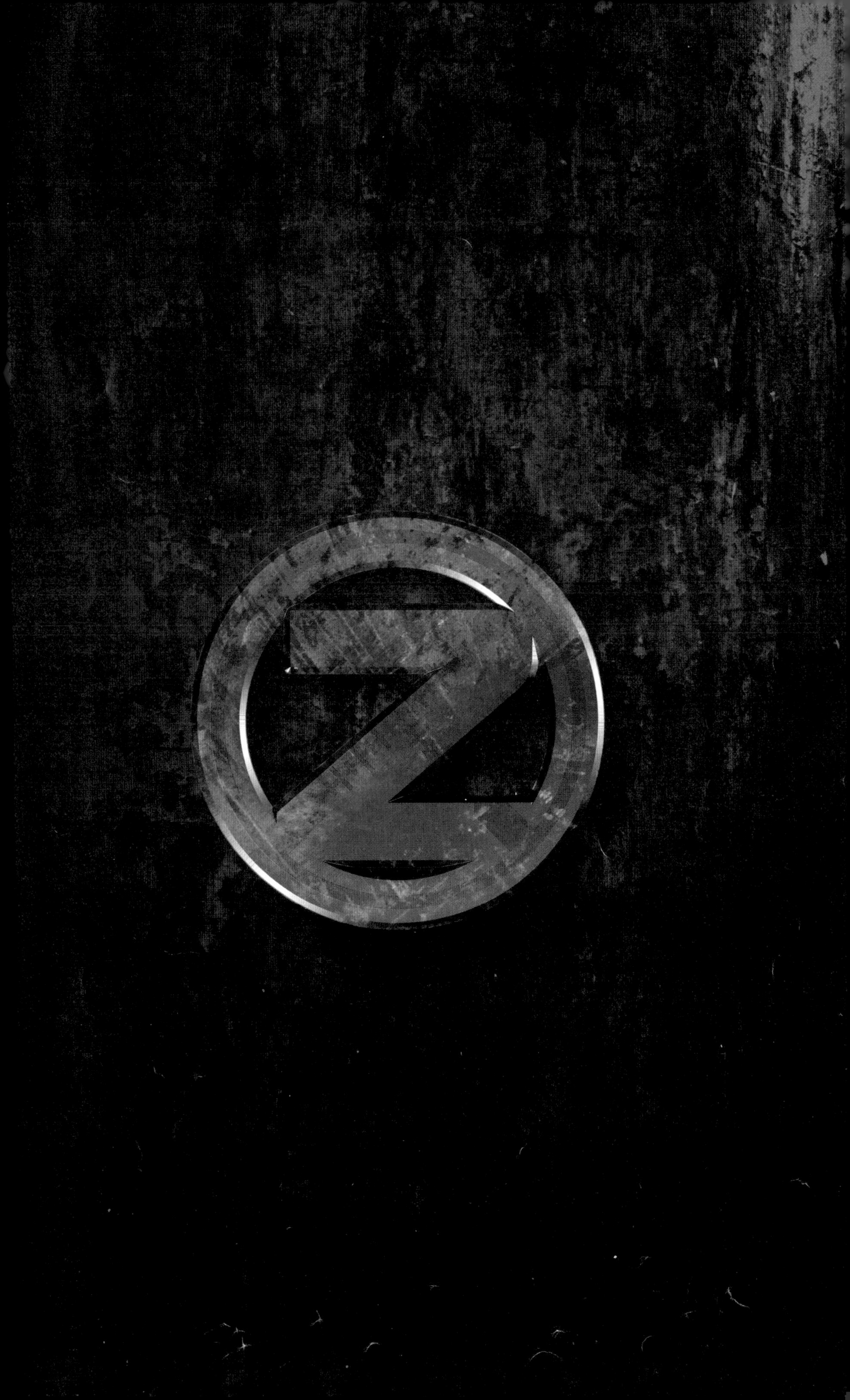

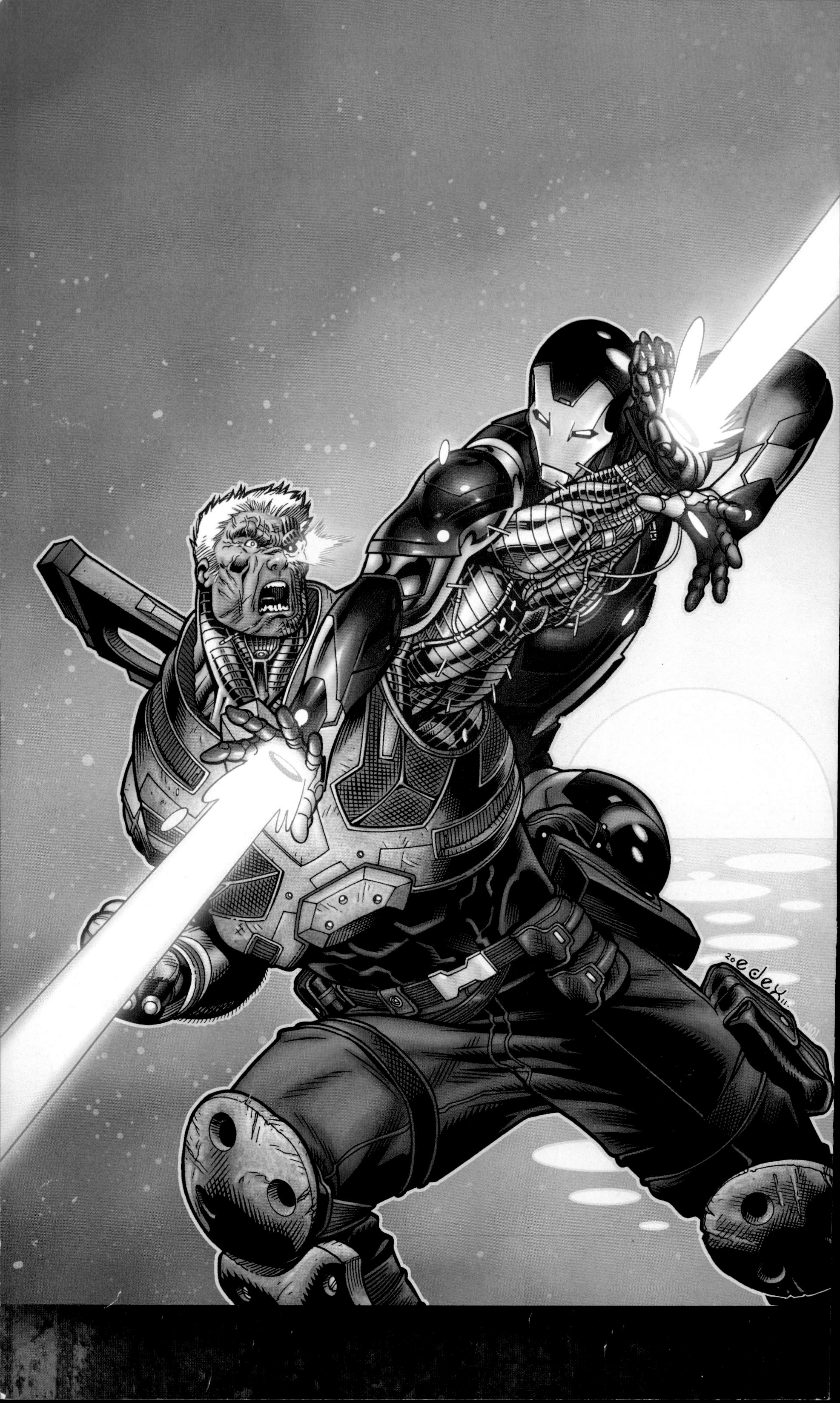

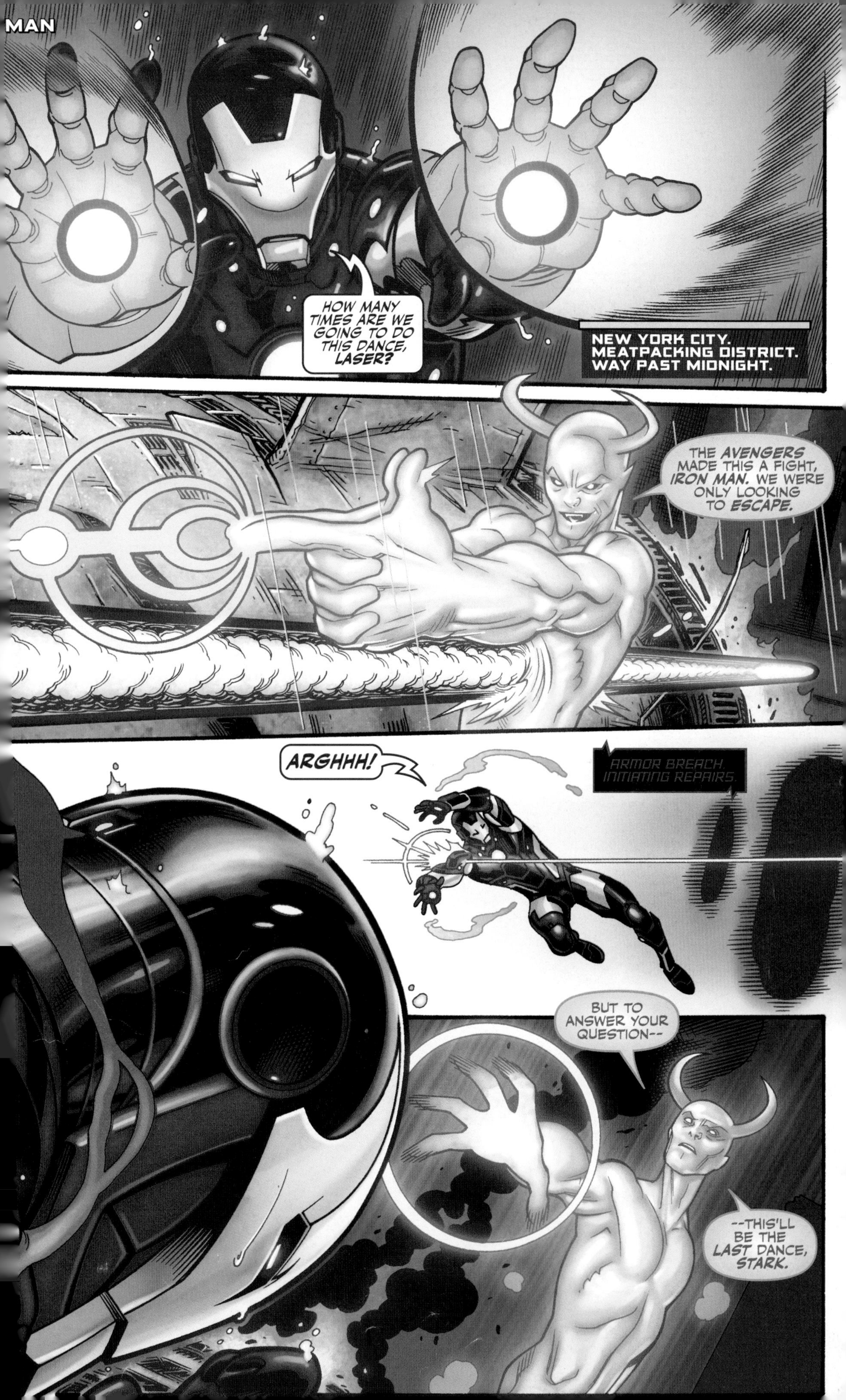
HOW MANY TIMES ARE WE GOING TO DO THIS DANCE, LASER?
NEW YORK CITY. MEATPACKING DISTRICT. WAY PAST MIDNIGHT.
THE AVENGERS MADE THIS A FIGHT, IRON MAN. WE WERE ONLY LOOKING TO ESCAPE.
ARGHHH!
ARMOR BREACH. INITIATING REPAIRS.
BUT TO ANSWER YOUR QUESTION--
--THIS'LL BE THE LAST DANCE, STARK.

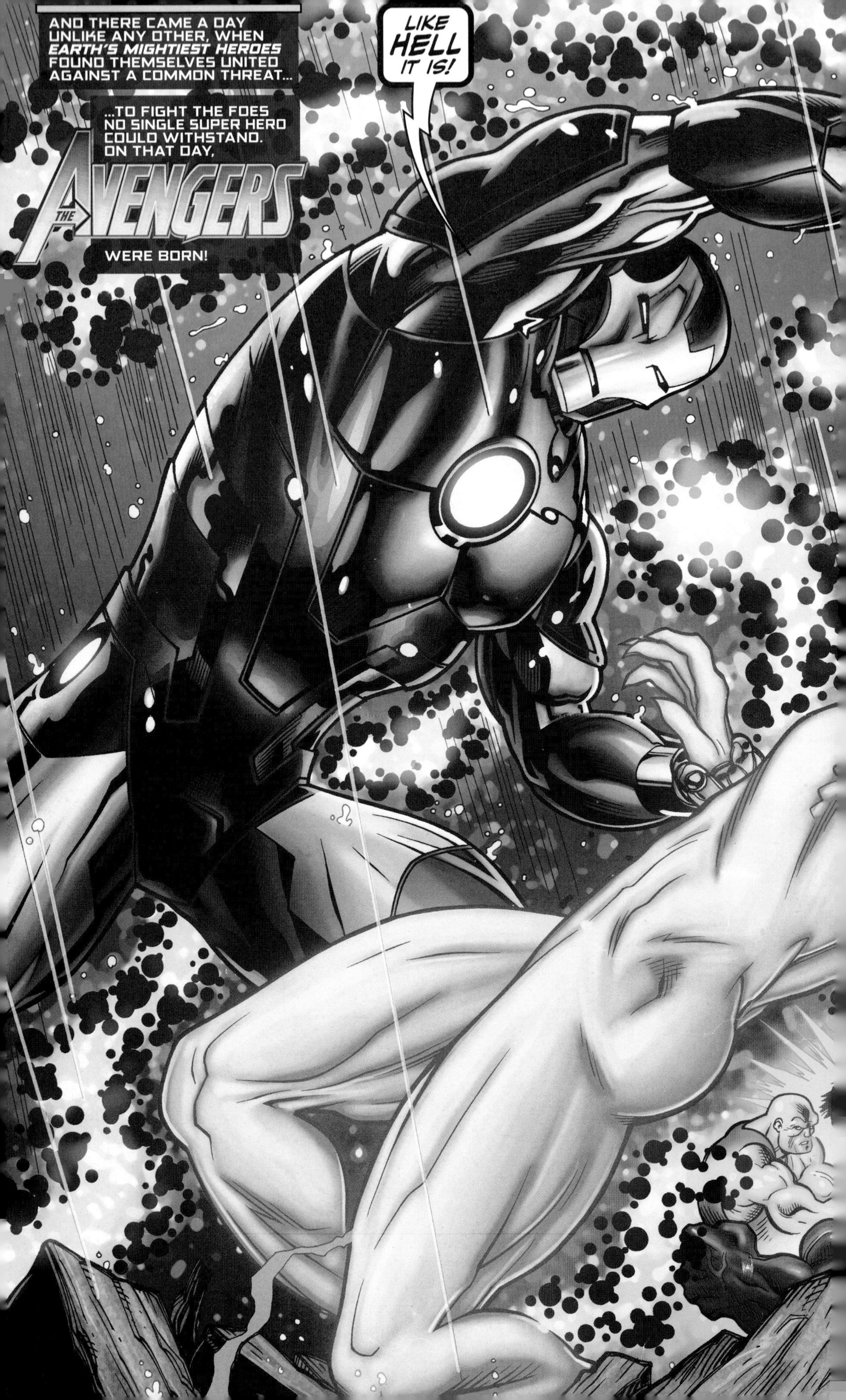
AND THERE CAME A DAY UNLIKE ANY OTHER, WHEN EARTH'S MIGHTIEST HEROES FOUND THEMSELVES UNITED AGAINST A COMMON THREAT...
LIKE HELL IT IS!
...TO FIGHT THE FOES NO SINGLE SUPER HERO COULD WITHSTAND. ON THAT DAY,
THE AVENGERS
WERE BORN!

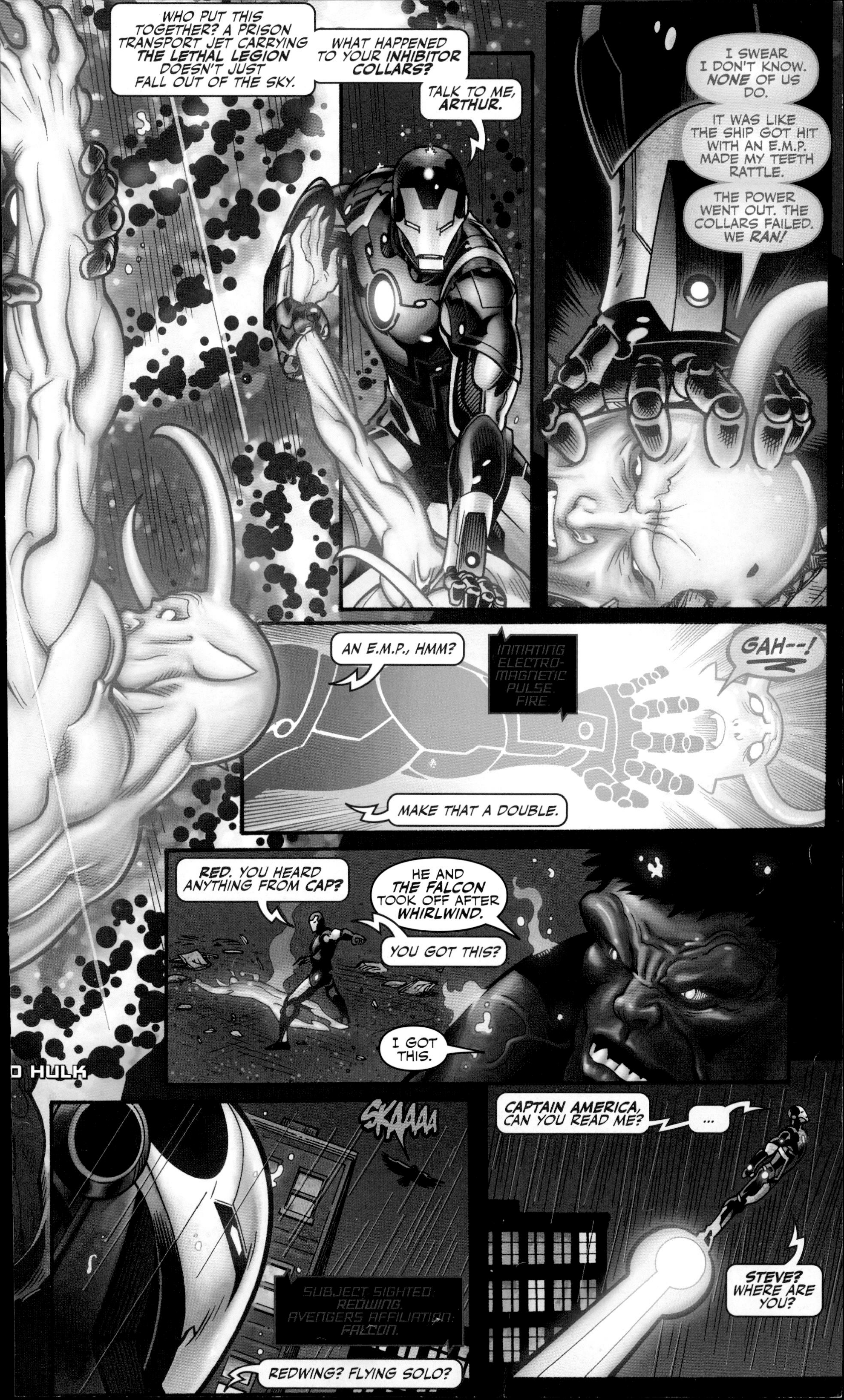
WHO PUT THIS TOGETHER? A PRISON TRANSPORT JET CARRYING THE LETHAL LEGION DOESN'T JUST FALL OUT OF THE SKY.
WHAT HAPPENED TO YOUR INHIBITOR COLLARS?
TALK TO ME, ARTHUR.
I SWEAR I DON'T KNOW. NONE OF US DO.
IT WAS LIKE THE SHIP GOT HIT WITH AN E.M.P. MADE MY TEETH RATTLE.
THE POWER WENT OUT. THE COLLARS FAILED. WE RAN!
AN E.M.P., HMM?
INITIATING ELECTRO-MAGNETIC PULSE. FIRE.
GAH--!
MAKE THAT A DOUBLE.
RED. YOU HEARD ANYTHING FROM CAP?
HE AND THE FALCON TOOK OFF AFTER WHIRLWIND.
YOU GOT THIS?
I GOT THIS.
D HULK
SKAAAA
SUBJECT SIGHTED: REDWING. AVENGERS AFFILIATION: FALCON.
REDWING? FLYING SOLO?
CAPTAIN AMERICA, CAN YOU READ ME?
...
STEVE? WHERE ARE YOU?

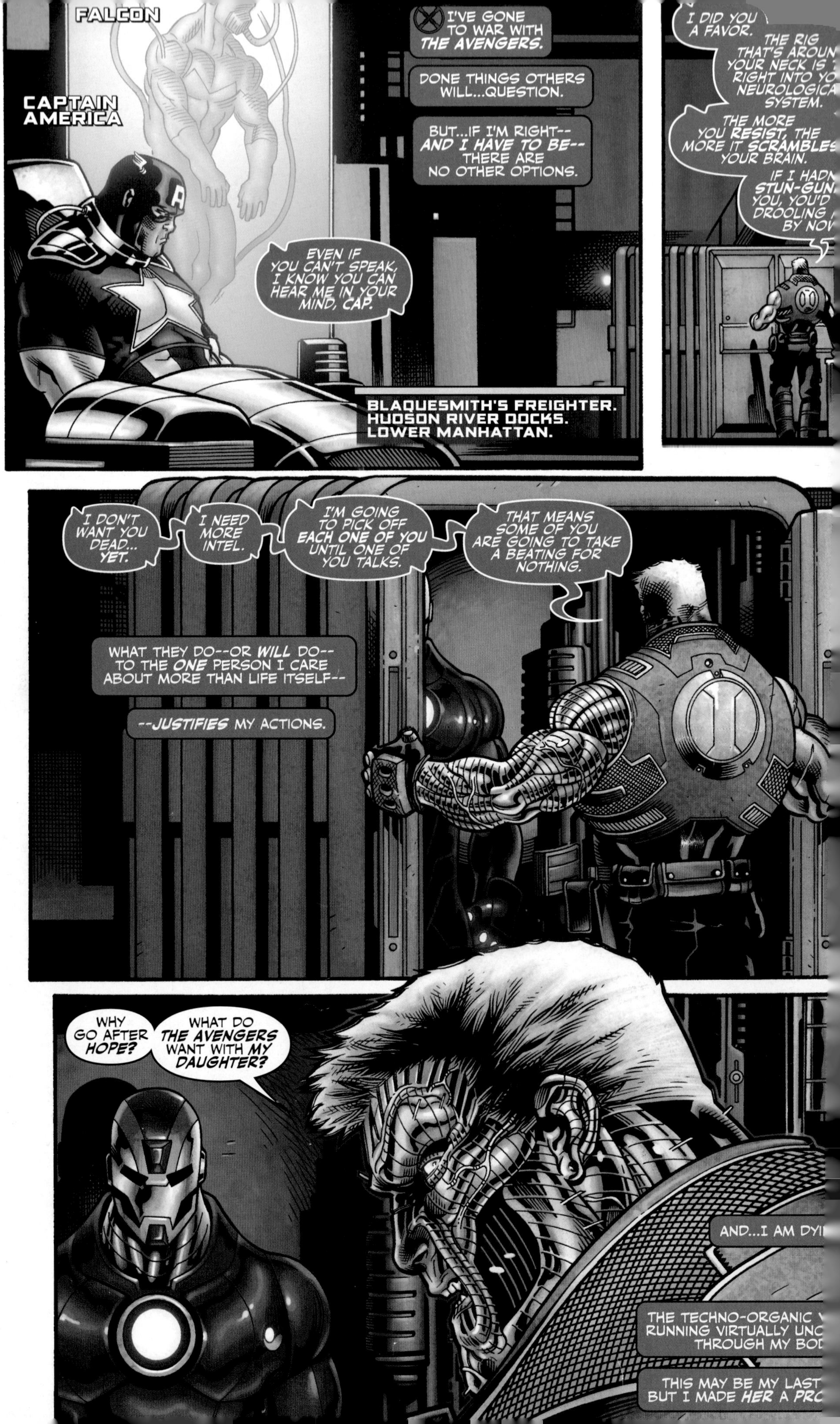
FALCON
CAPTAIN AMERICA
I'VE GONE TO WAR WITH THE AVENGERS.
DONE THINGS OTHERS WILL...QUESTION.
BUT...IF I'M RIGHT-- AND I HAVE TO BE-- THERE ARE NO OTHER OPTIONS.
EVEN IF YOU CAN'T SPEAK, I KNOW YOU CAN HEAR ME IN YOUR MIND, CAP.
BLAQUESMITH'S FREIGHTER. HUDSON RIVER DOCKS. LOWER MANHATTAN.
I DID YOU A FAVOR.
THE RIG THAT'S AROUN YOUR NECK IS RIGHT INTO YO NEUROLOGICA SYSTEM.
THE MORE YOU RESIST, THE MORE IT SCRAMBLES YOUR BRAIN.
IF I HADN STUN-GUN YOU, YOU'D DROOLING BY NOV
I DON'T WANT YOU DEAD... YET.
I NEED MORE INTEL.
I'M GOING TO PICK OFF EACH ONE OF YOU UNTIL ONE OF YOU TALKS.
THAT MEANS SOME OF YOU ARE GOING TO TAKE A BEATING FOR NOTHING.
WHAT THEY DO--OR WILL DO-- TO THE ONE PERSON I CARE ABOUT MORE THAN LIFE ITSELF--
--JUSTIFIES MY ACTIONS.
WHY GO AFTER HOPE?
WHAT DO THE AVENGERS WANT WITH MY DAUGHTER?
AND...I AM DYI
THE TECHNO-ORGANIC RUNNING VIRTUALLY UNC THROUGH MY BOD
THIS MAY BE MY LAST BUT I MADE HER A PRO

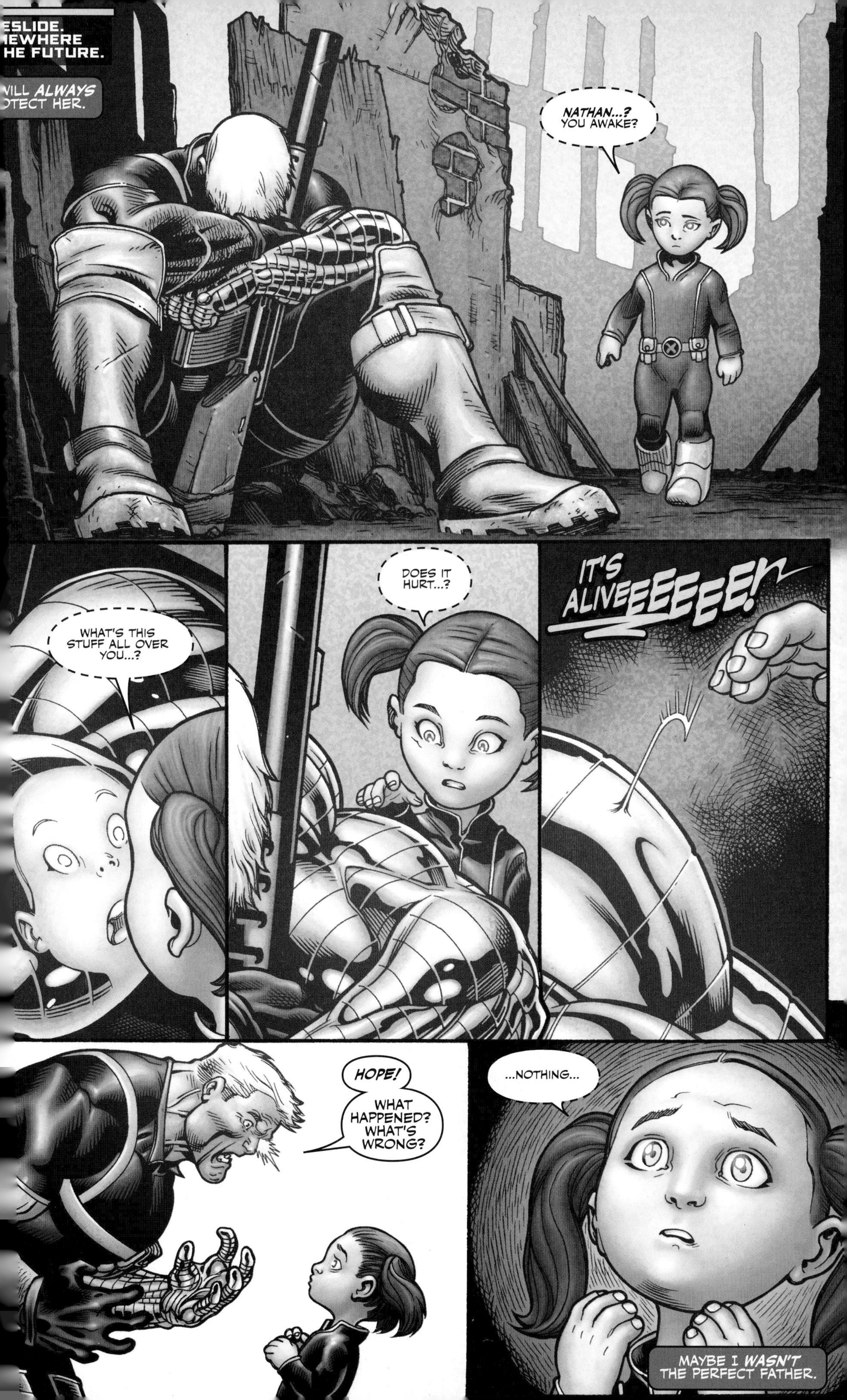

ESLIDE.
EWHERE
HE FUTURE.
VILL ALWAYS
OTECT HER.
NATHAN...? YOU AWAKE?
WHAT'S THIS STUFF ALL OVER YOU...?
DOES IT HURT...?
IT'S ALIVEEEEEEE!
HOPE!
WHAT HAPPENED? WHAT'S WRONG?
...NOTHING...
MAYBE I WASN'T THE PERFECT FATHER.

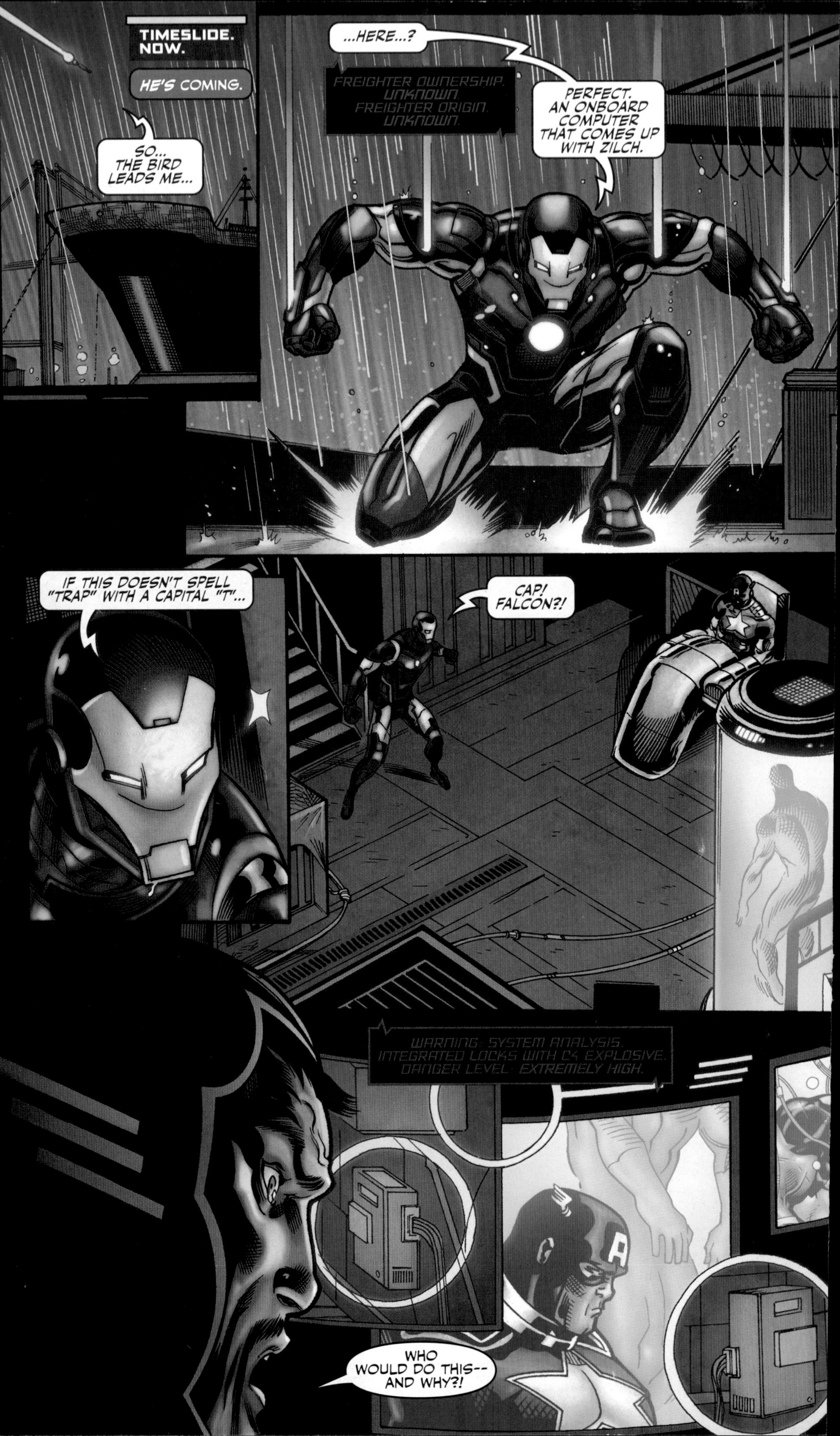
TIMESLIDE. NOW.
HE'S COMING.
SO... THE BIRD LEADS ME...
...HERE...?
FREIGHTER OWNERSHIP. UNKNOWN. FREIGHTER ORIGIN. UNKNOWN.
PERFECT. AN ONBOARD COMPUTER THAT COMES UP WITH ZILCH.
IF THIS DOESN'T SPELL "TRAP" WITH A CAPITAL "T"...
CAP! FALCON?!
WARNING: SYSTEM ANALYSIS. INTEGRATED LOCKS WITH C4 EXPLOSIVE. DANGER LEVEL: EXTREMELY HIGH.
WHO WOULD DO THIS-- AND WHY?!

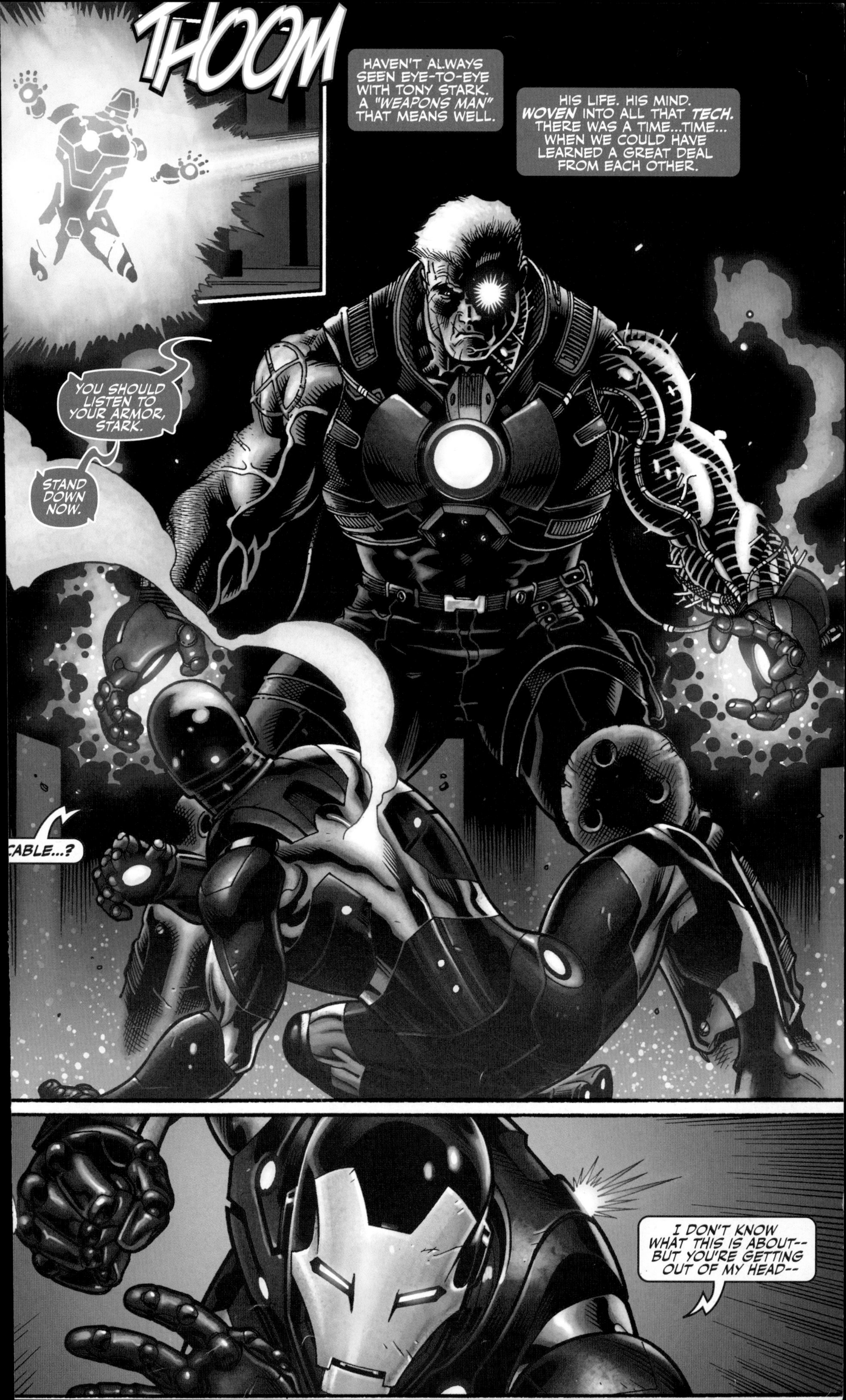
THOOM
HAVEN'T ALWAYS SEEN EYE-TO-EYE WITH TONY STARK. A "WEAPONS MAN" THAT MEANS WELL.
HIS LIFE. HIS MIND. WOVEN INTO ALL THAT TECH. THERE WAS A TIME...TIME... WHEN WE COULD HAVE LEARNED A GREAT DEAL FROM EACH OTHER.
YOU SHOULD LISTEN TO YOUR ARMOR, STARK.
STAND DOWN NOW.
CABLE...?
I DON'T KNOW WHAT THIS IS ABOUT-- BUT YOU'RE GETTING OUT OF MY HEAD--

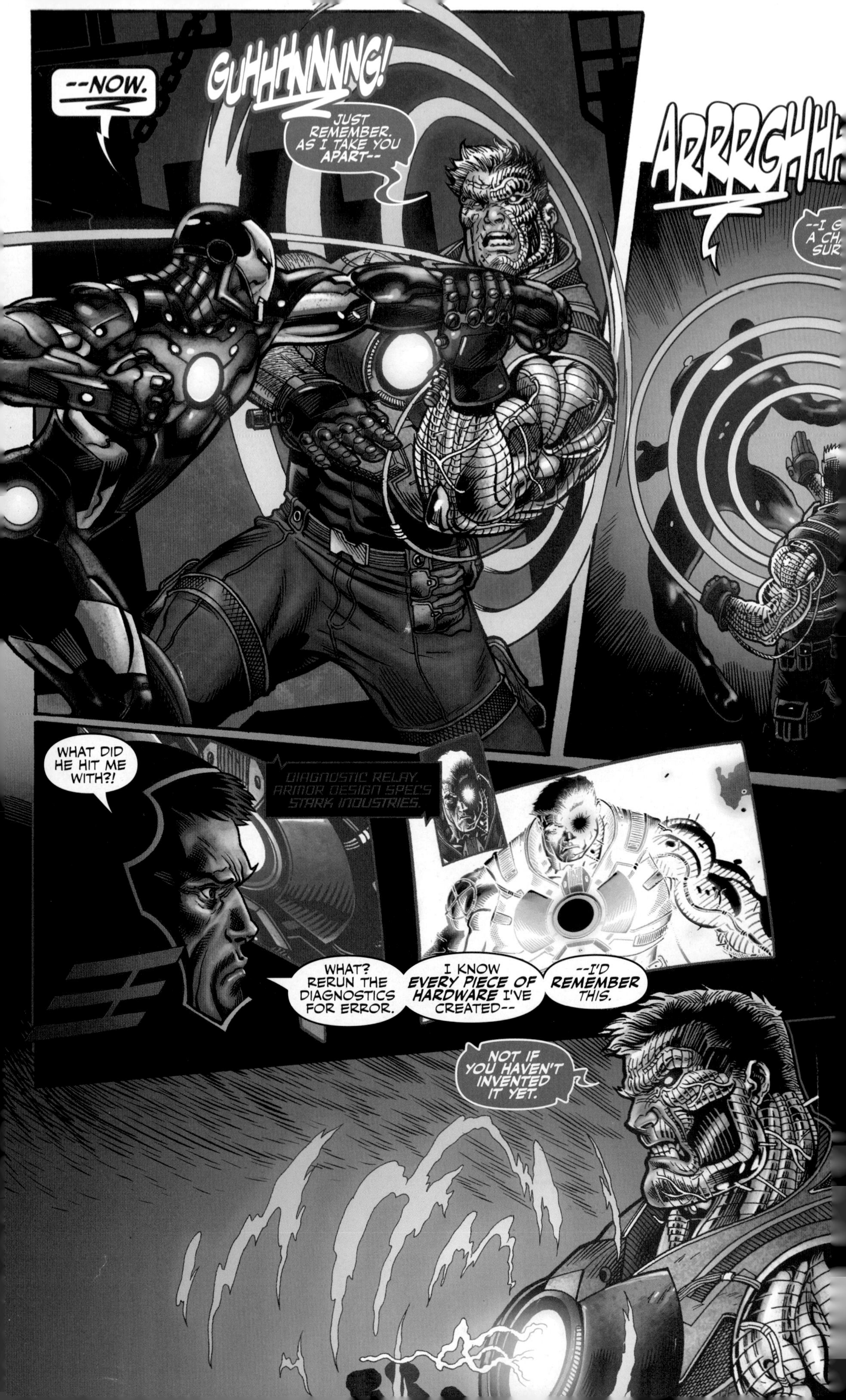
--NOW.
GUHHHNNNNG!
JUST REMEMBER. AS I TAKE YOU APART--
WHAT DID HE HIT ME WITH?!
DIAGNOSTIC RELAY. ARMOR DESIGN SPECS STARK INDUSTRIES.
WHAT? RERUN THE DIAGNOSTICS FOR ERROR.
I KNOW EVERY PIECE OF HARDWARE I'VE CREATED--
--I'D REMEMBER THIS.
NOT IF YOU HAVEN'T INVENTED IT YET.

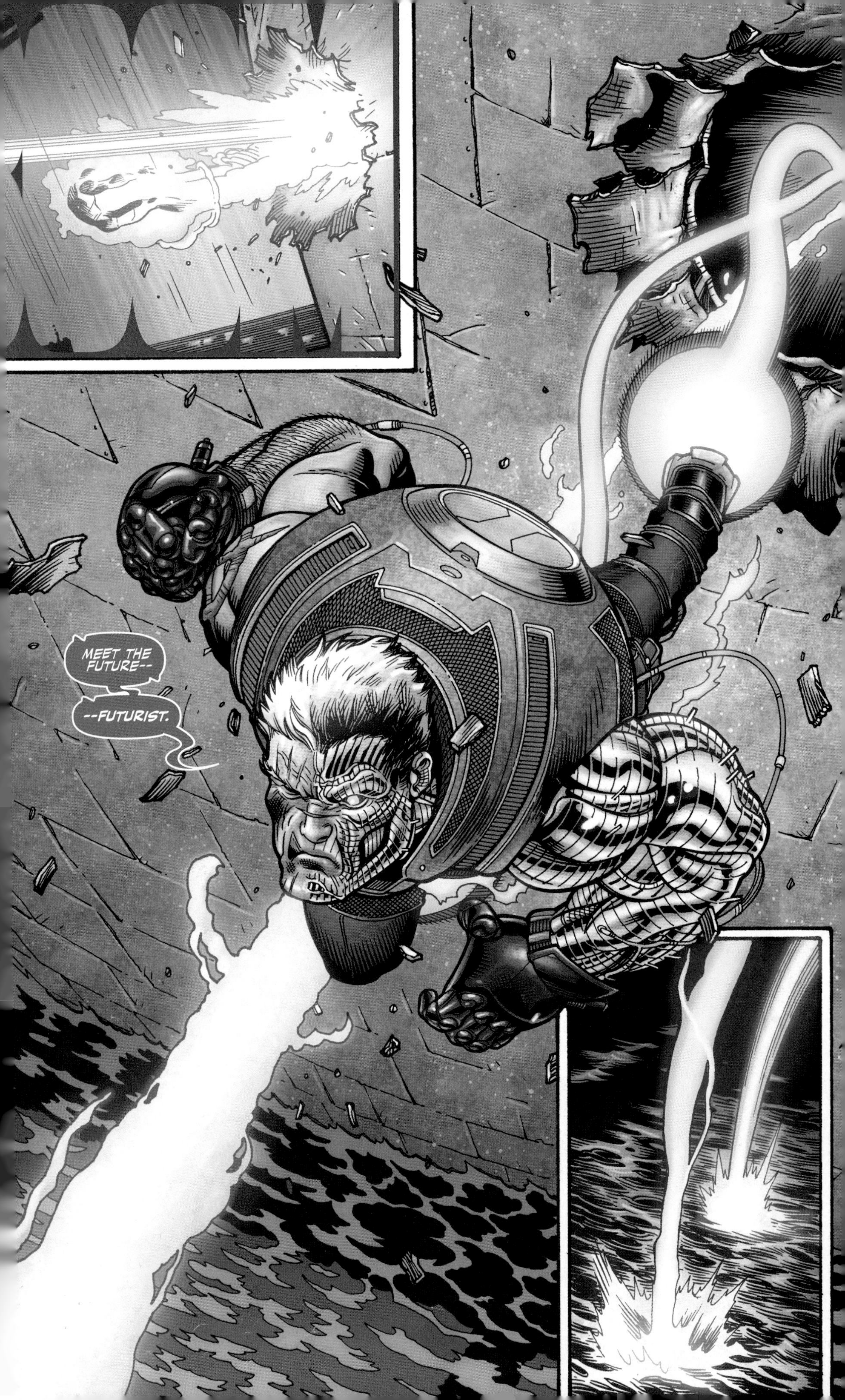
MEET THE FUTURE--
--FUTURIST.

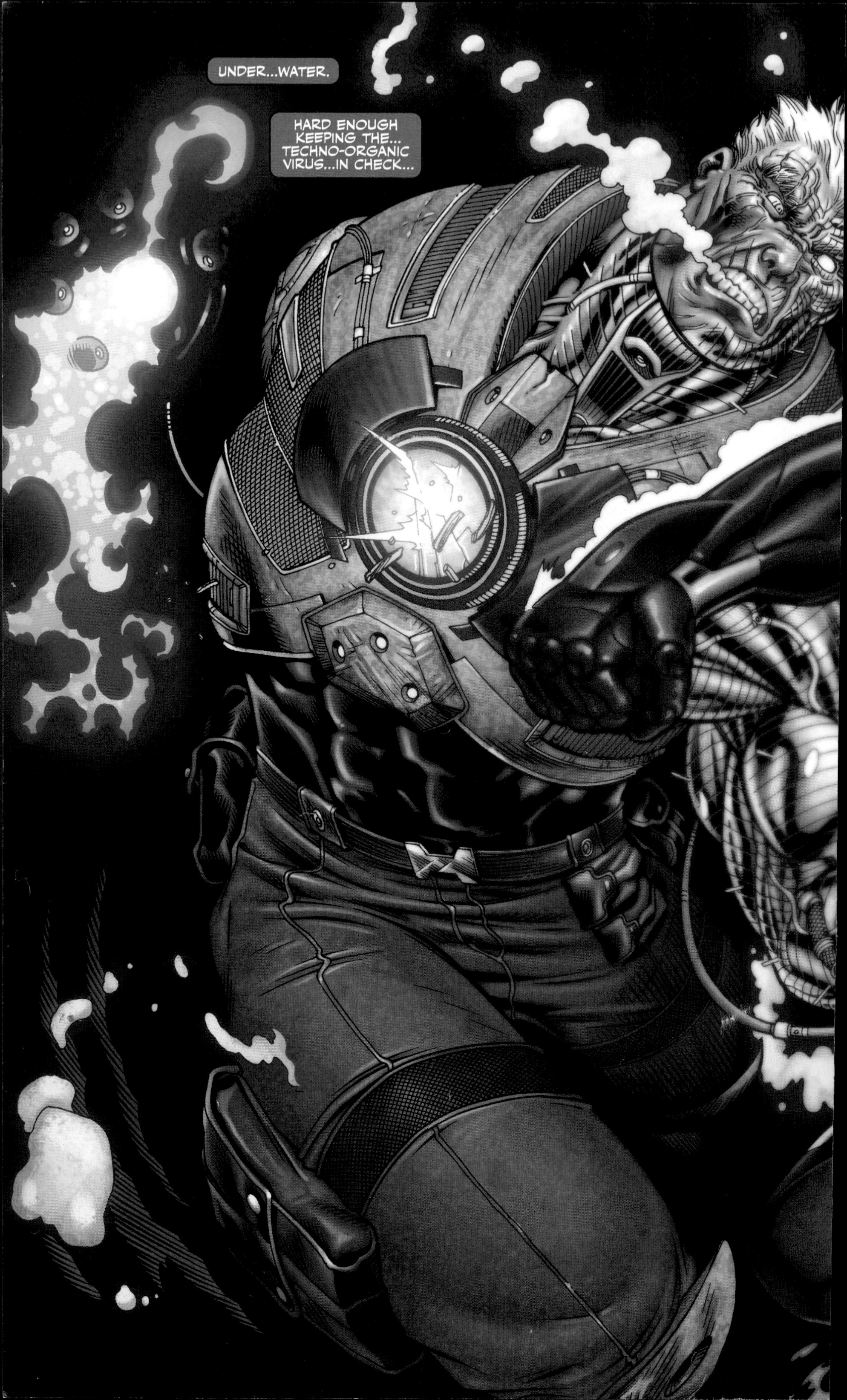
UNDER...WATER.
HARD ENOUGH KEEPING THE... TECHNO-ORGANIC VIRUS...IN CHECK...

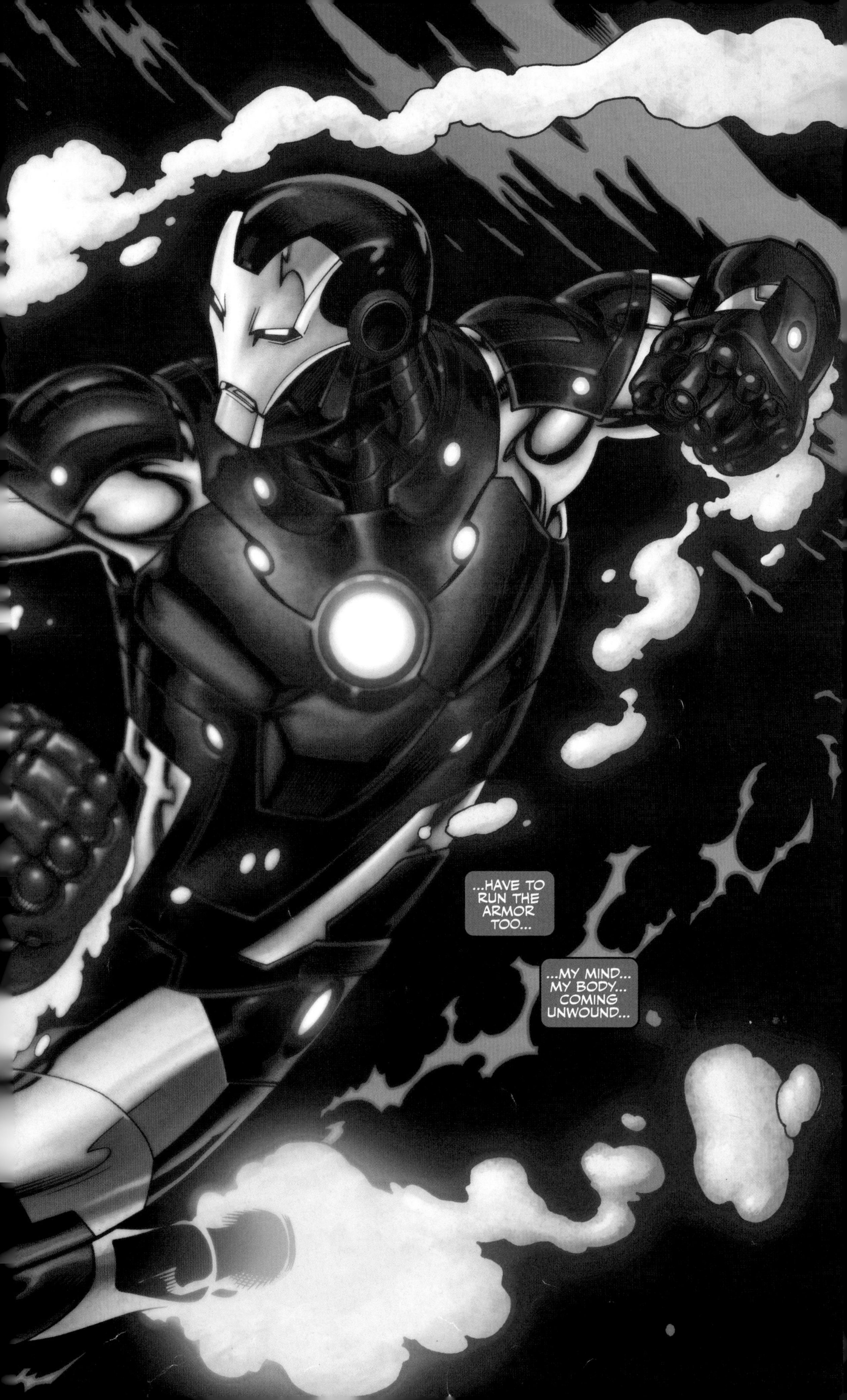
...HAVE TO RUN THE ARMOR TOO...
...MY MIND... MY BODY... COMING UNWOUND...

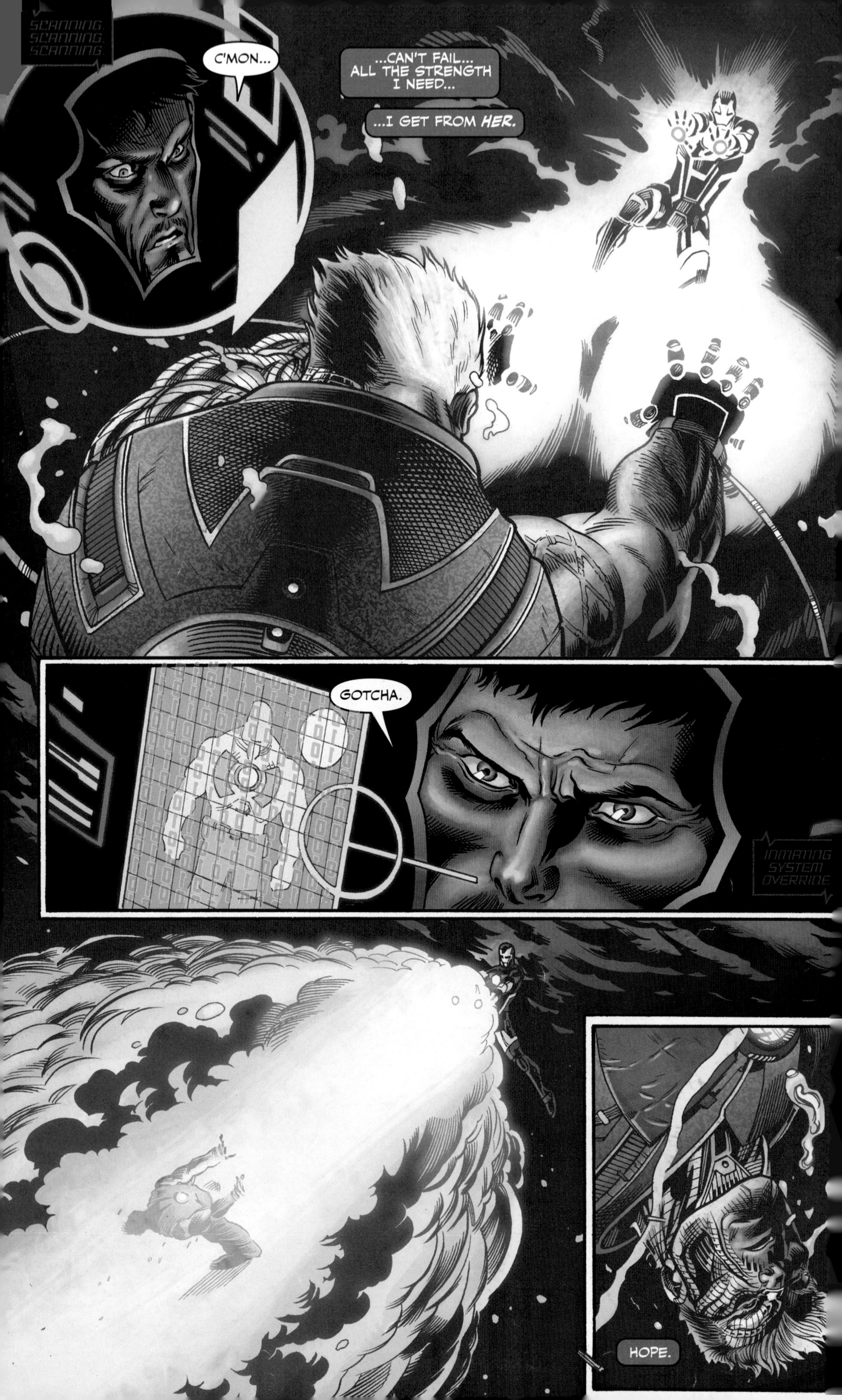
SCANNING.
SCANNING.
SCANNING.
C'MON...
...CAN'T FAIL... ALL THE STRENGTH I NEED...
...I GET FROM HER.
GOTCHA.
INNATING SYSTEM OVERRIDE
HOPE.

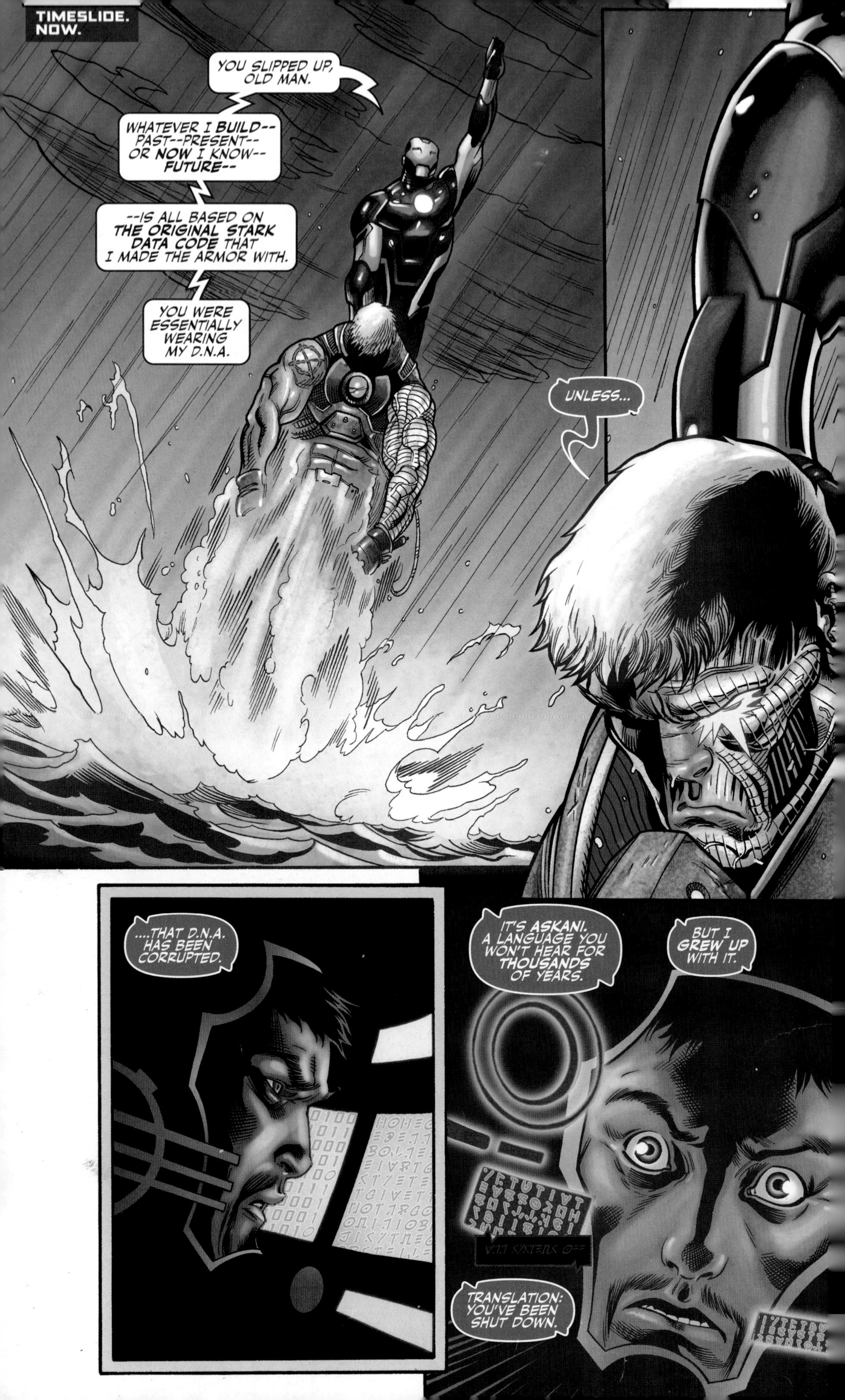
TIMESLIDE. NOW.
YOU SLIPPED UP, OLD MAN.
WHATEVER I BUILD-- PAST--PRESENT-- OR NOW I KNOW-- FUTURE--
--IS ALL BASED ON THE ORIGINAL STARK DATA CODE THAT I MADE THE ARMOR WITH.
YOU WERE ESSENTIALLY WEARING MY D.N.A.
UNLESS...
....THAT D.N.A. HAS BEEN CORRUPTED.
IT'S ASKANI. A LANGUAGE YOU WON'T HEAR FOR THOUSANDS OF YEARS.
BUT I GREW UP WITH IT.
TRANSLATION: YOU'VE BEEN SHUT DOWN.

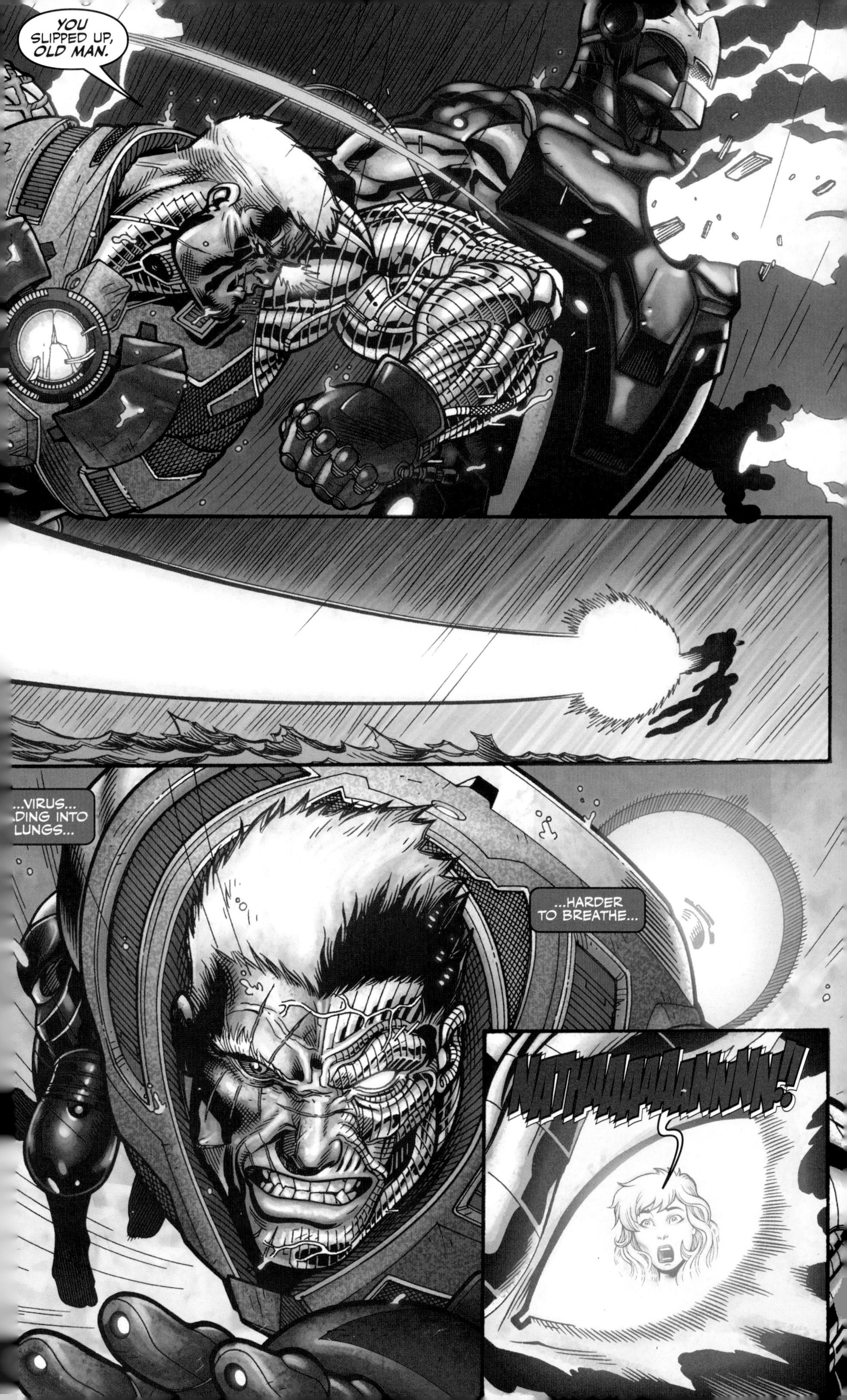

YOU SLIPPED UP, OLD MAN.
...VIRUS... DING INTO LUNGS...
...HARDER TO BREATHE...
NATHAAAAAANNNN!!

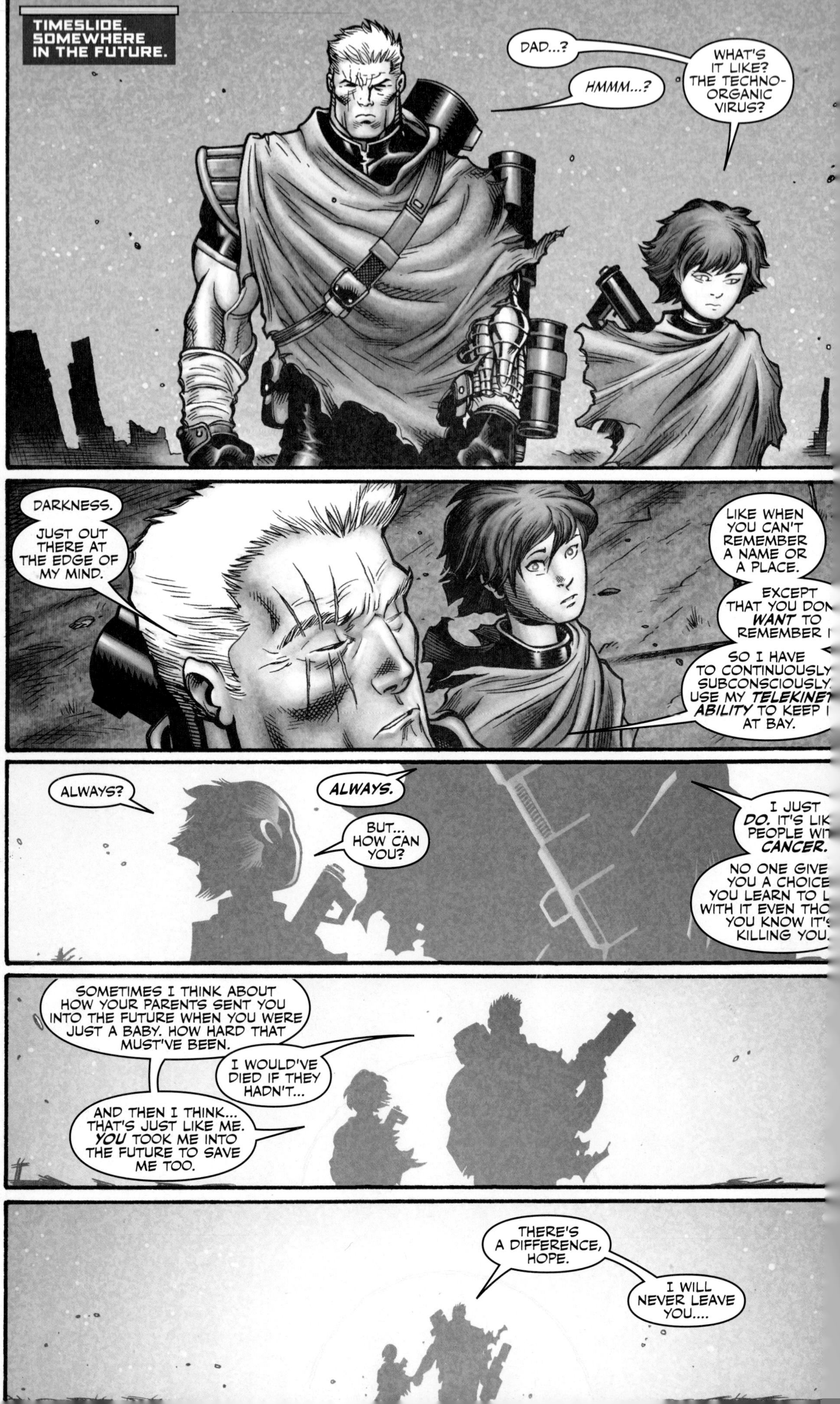
TIMESLIDE. SOMEWHERE IN THE FUTURE.
DAD...?
HMMM...?
WHAT'S IT LIKE? THE TECHNO-ORGANIC VIRUS?
DARKNESS.
JUST OUT THERE AT THE EDGE OF MY MIND.
LIKE WHEN YOU CAN'T REMEMBER A NAME OR A PLACE.
EXCEPT THAT YOU DON WANT TO REMEMBER I
SO I HAVE TO CONTINUOUSLY SUBCONSCIOUSLY USE MY TELEKINET ABILITY TO KEEP I AT BAY.
ALWAYS?
ALWAYS.
BUT... HOW CAN YOU?
I JUST DO. IT'S LIK PEOPLE WIT CANCER.
NO ONE GIVE YOU A CHOICE YOU LEARN TO L WITH IT EVEN THO YOU KNOW IT'S KILLING YOU.
SOMETIMES I THINK ABOUT HOW YOUR PARENTS SENT YOU INTO THE FUTURE WHEN YOU WERE JUST A BABY. HOW HARD THAT MUST'VE BEEN.
I WOULD'VE DIED IF THEY HADN'T...
AND THEN I THINK... THAT'S JUST LIKE ME. YOU TOOK ME INTO THE FUTURE TO SAVE ME TOO.
THERE'S A DIFFERENCE, HOPE.
I WILL NEVER LEAVE YOU....

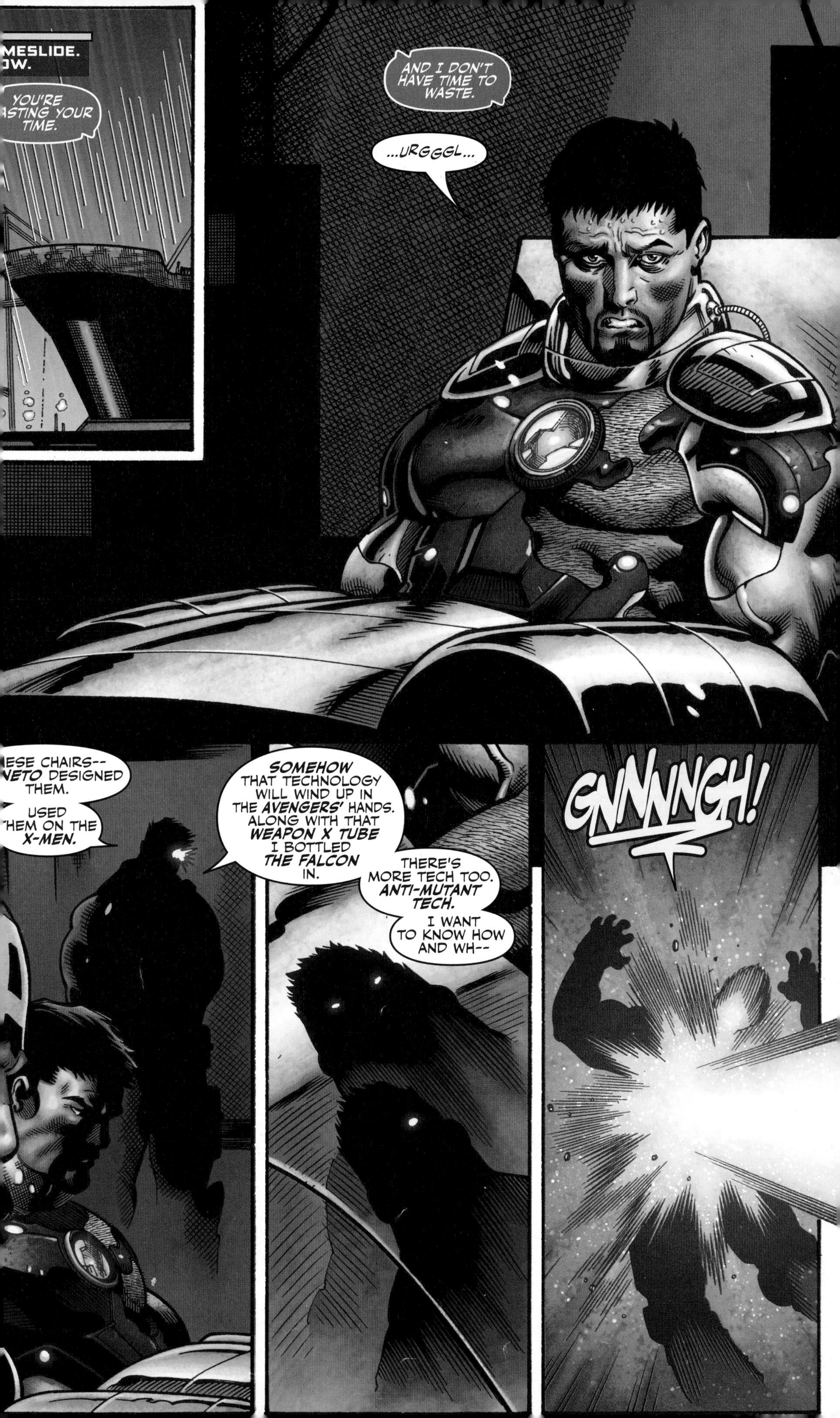

MESLIDE.
OW.
YOU'RE
ASTING YOUR
TIME.
AND I DON'T HAVE TIME TO WASTE.
...URGGGL...
ESE CHAIRS--
NETO DESIGNED THEM.
USED
THEM ON THE X-MEN.
SOMEHOW THAT TECHNOLOGY WILL WIND UP IN THE AVENGERS' HANDS. ALONG WITH THAT WEAPON X TUBE I BOTTLED THE FALCON IN.
THERE'S MORE TECH TOO. ANTI-MUTANT TECH.
I WANT TO KNOW HOW AND WH--
GNNNNGH!

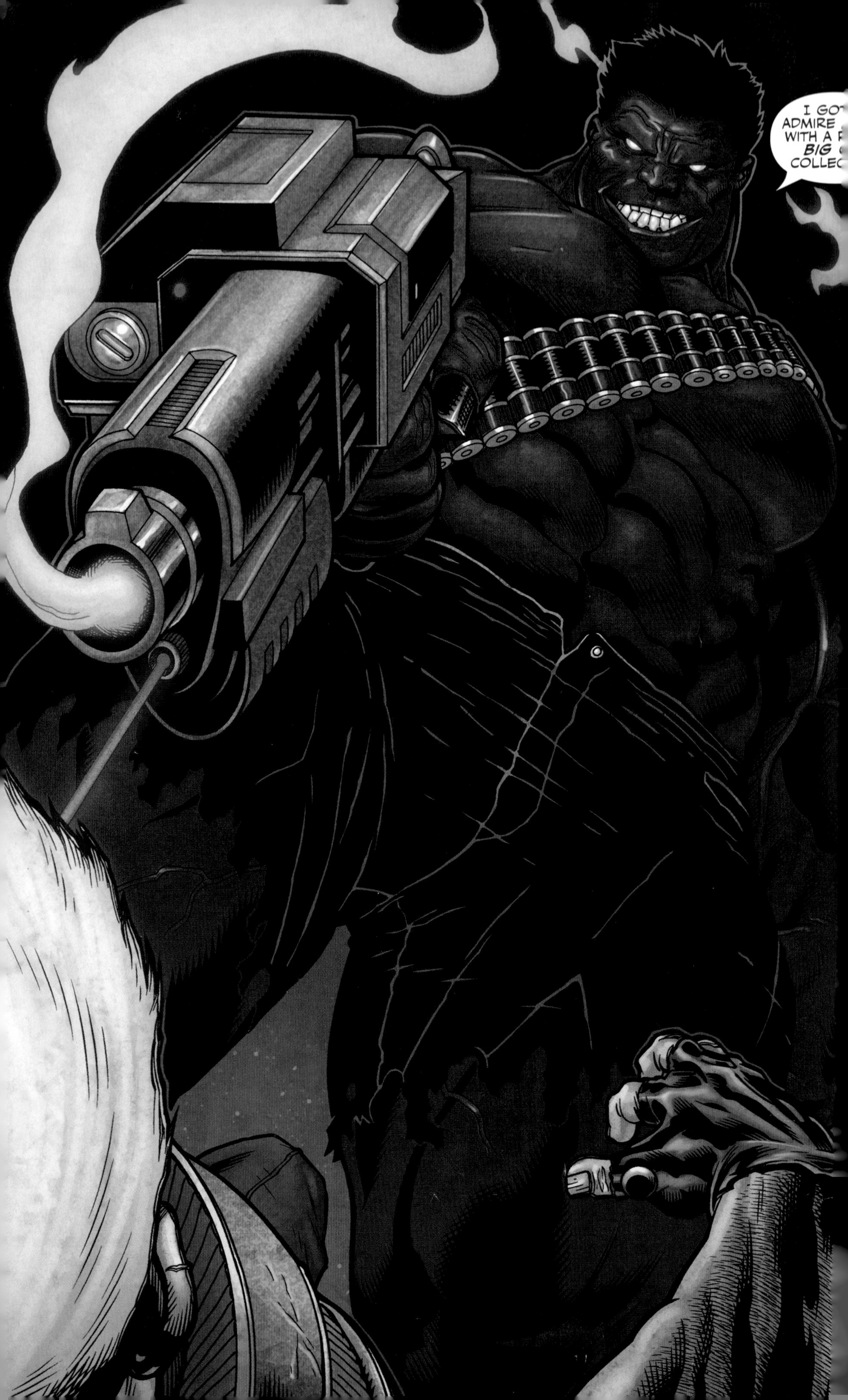
I GO
ADMIRE
WITH A
BIG
COLLE

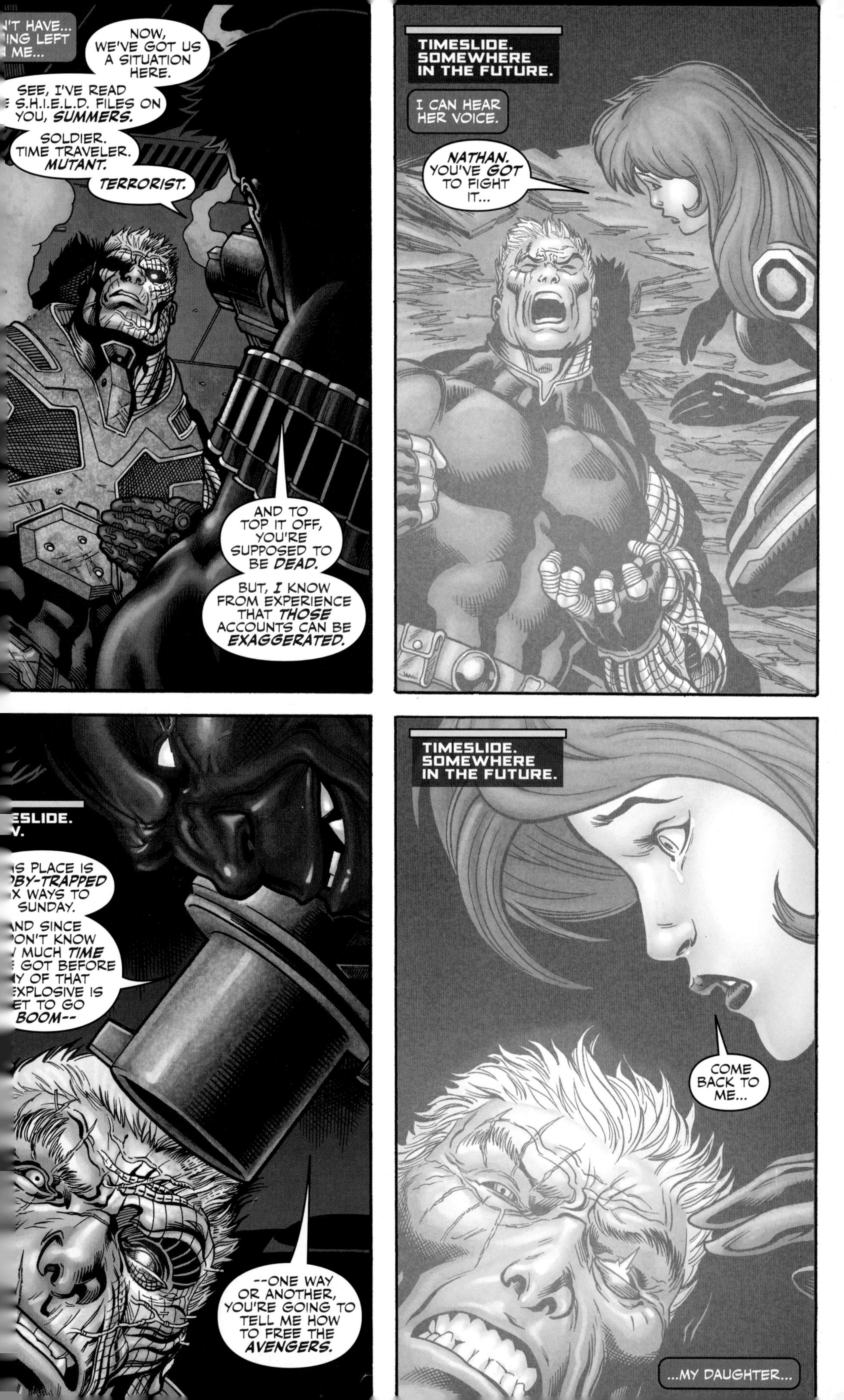N'T HAVE... ING LEFT ME...
NOW, WE'VE GOT US A SITUATION HERE.
SEE, I'VE READ S.H.I.E.L.D. FILES ON YOU, SUMMERS.
SOLDIER. TIME TRAVELER. MUTANT.
TERRORIST.
AND TO TOP IT OFF, YOU'RE SUPPOSED TO BE DEAD.
BUT, I KNOW FROM EXPERIENCE THAT THOSE ACCOUNTS CAN BE EXAGGERATED.
TIMESLIDE. SOMEWHERE IN THE FUTURE.
I CAN HEAR HER VOICE.
NATHAN. YOU'VE GOT TO FIGHT IT...
ESLIDE.
IS PLACE IS OBY-TRAPPED X WAYS TO SUNDAY.
AND SINCE ON'T KNOW MUCH TIME GOT BEFORE Y OF THAT EXPLOSIVE IS ET TO GO BOOM--
--ONE WAY OR ANOTHER, YOU'RE GOING TO TELL ME HOW TO FREE THE AVENGERS.
TIMESLIDE. SOMEWHERE IN THE FUTURE.
COME BACK TO ME...
...MY DAUGHTER...

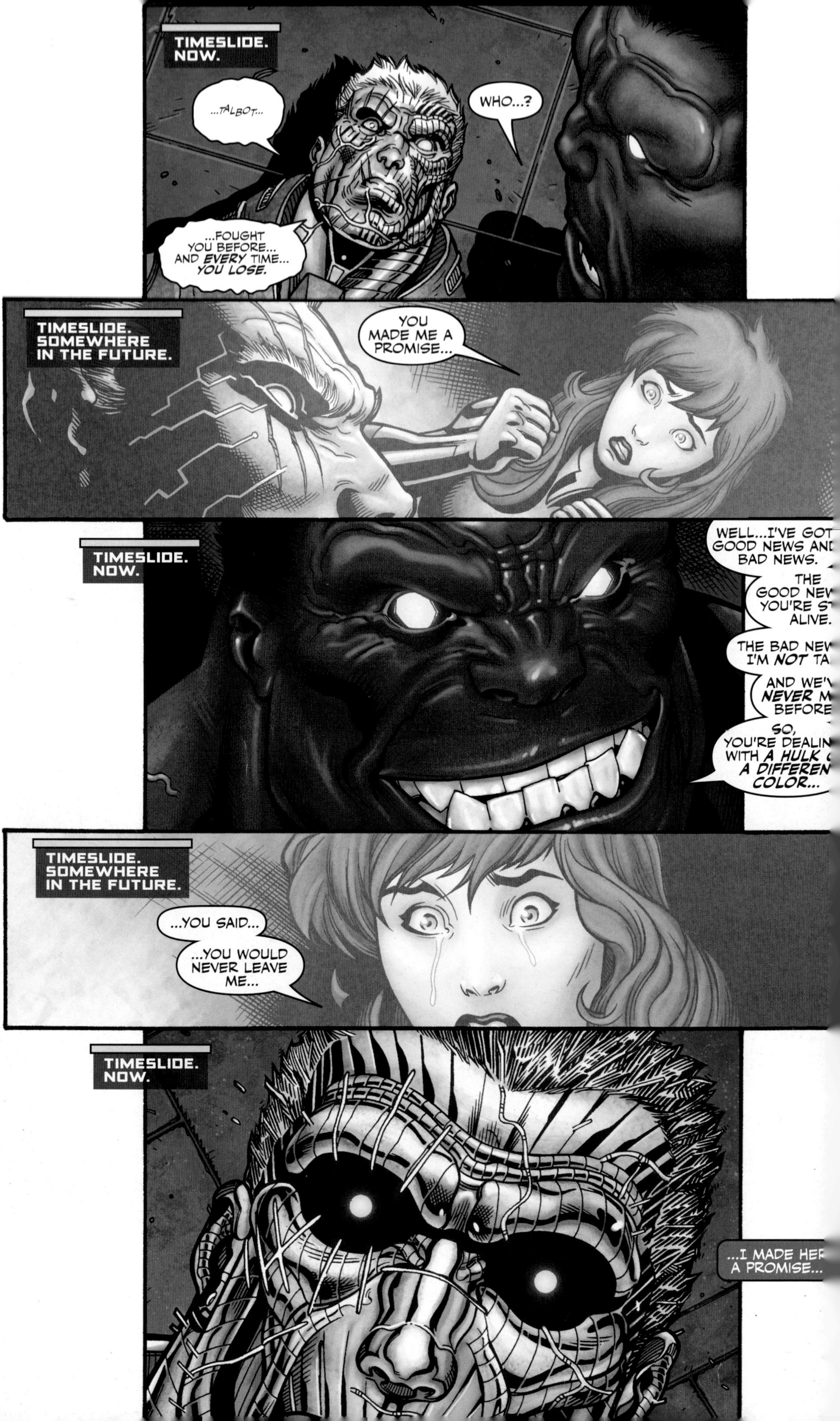

TIMESLIDE. NOW.
...TALBOT...
WHO...?
...FOUGHT YOU BEFORE... AND EVERY TIME... YOU LOSE.
TIMESLIDE. SOMEWHERE IN THE FUTURE.
YOU MADE ME A PROMISE...
TIMESLIDE. NOW.
WELL...I'VE GOT GOOD NEWS AND BAD NEWS.
THE GOOD NEW YOU'RE ST ALIVE.
THE BAD NEW I'M NOT TA
AND WE'V NEVER M BEFORE
SO, YOU'RE DEALIN WITH A HULK A DIFFEREN COLOR...
TIMESLIDE. SOMEWHERE IN THE FUTURE.
...YOU SAID...
...YOU WOULD NEVER LEAVE ME...
TIMESLIDE. NOW.
...I MADE HER A PROMISE...

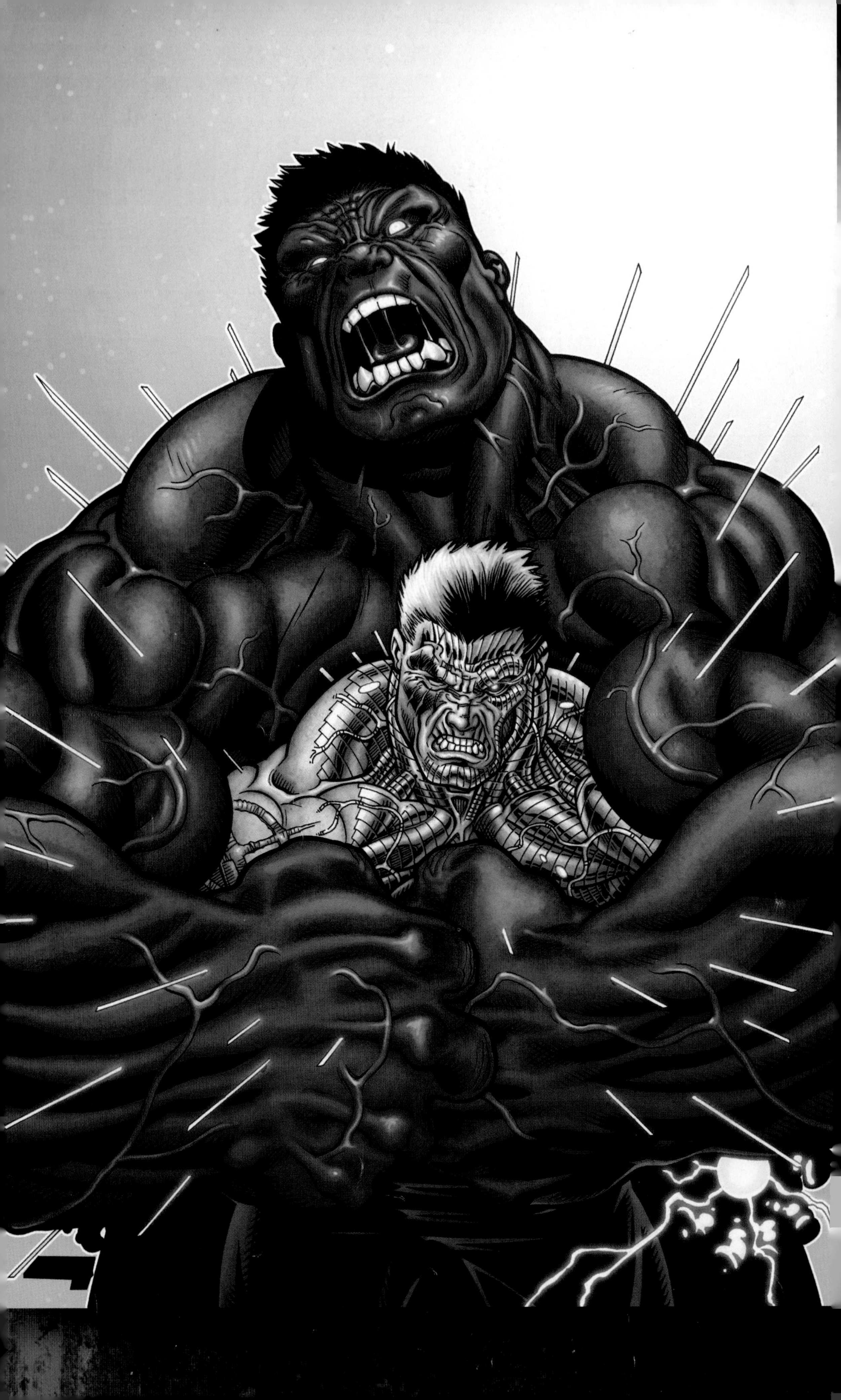

BLAQUESMITH'S FREIGHTER.
HUDSON RIVER DOCKS.
LOWER MANHATTAN.

THE PLAN INCLUDED TAKING OUT *THE RED HULK*. JUST NOT...*YET*.

THERE YOU GO AGAIN, *CABLE*.

CALLIN' ME *"TALBOT."*

GLENN TALBOT WAS A GOOD SOLDIER.

AND A *DEAD* MAN.

GUESS IT ≠KOFF≠ DEPENDS ON *WHEN* YOU'RE FROM THEN.

LET'S CUT TO IT.

YOU PULL THAT TRIGGER AND FOR ALL YOU KNOW YOUR *AVENGER* FRIENDS ALL DIE.

YOU WILLING TO ≠ARGH≠ TAKE THAT RISK?

...FF TAKE EST... T.

GONE TO WAR HE AVENGERS.

ITH LESS THAN E HOURS TO LIVE, E MISSION IS NRAVELING.

ODY HAS AYED ME. TECHNO- ANIC VIRUS ED WITH SINCE CY RAGES. TOPPABLE.

FIRE

ARE YOU?

TALBOT OR NOT, *THIS* HULK KNOWS WEAPONS. HE *THINKS* LIKE A MILITARY MAN.

JUST LIKE I DO. SO I'M SURE HE'LL APPRECIATE...

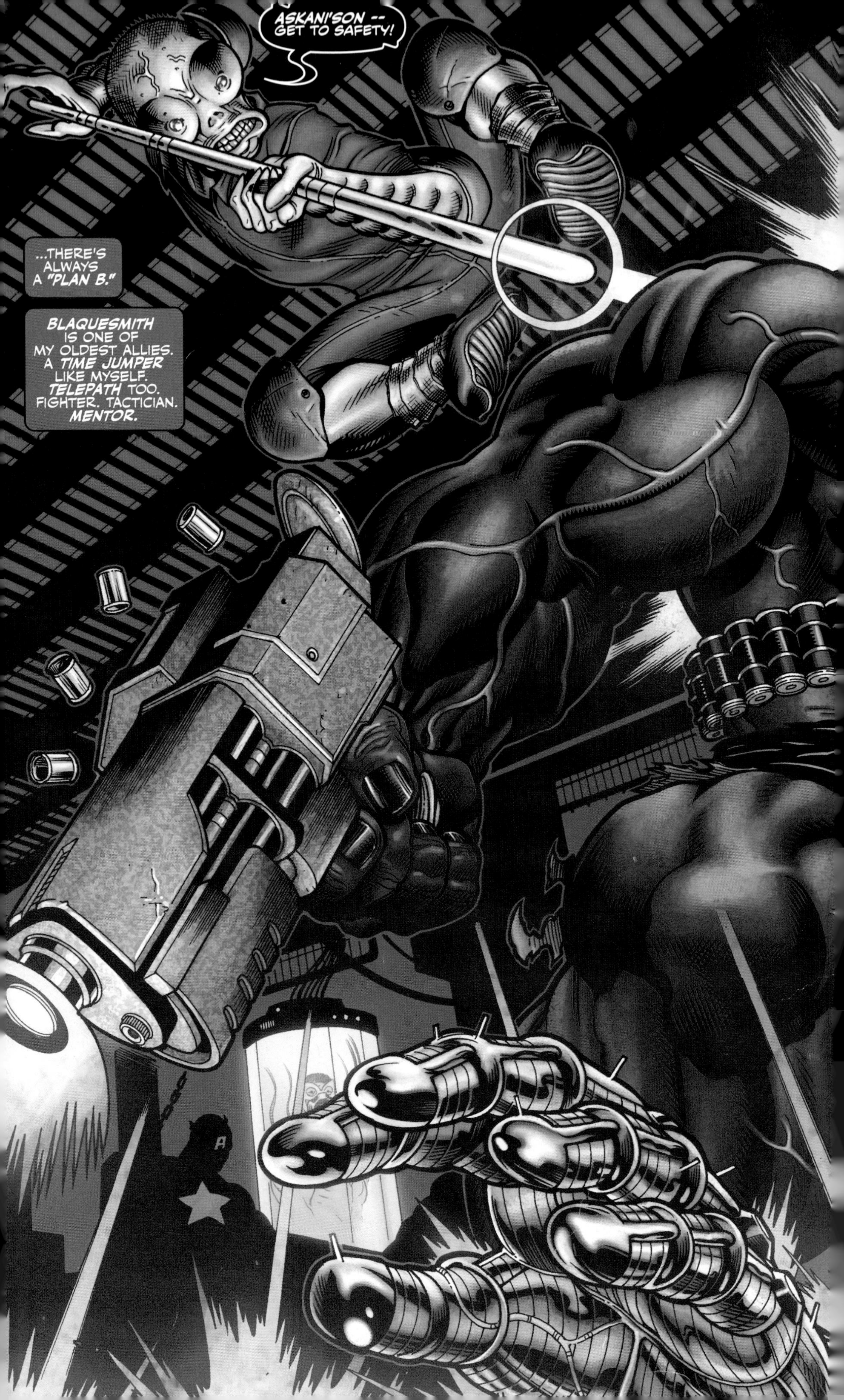
ASKANI'SON -- GET TO SAFETY!
...THERE'S ALWAYS A "PLAN B."
BLAQUESMITH IS ONE OF MY OLDEST ALLIES. A TIME JUMPER LIKE MYSELF. TELEPATH TOO. FIGHTER. TACTICIAN. MENTOR.

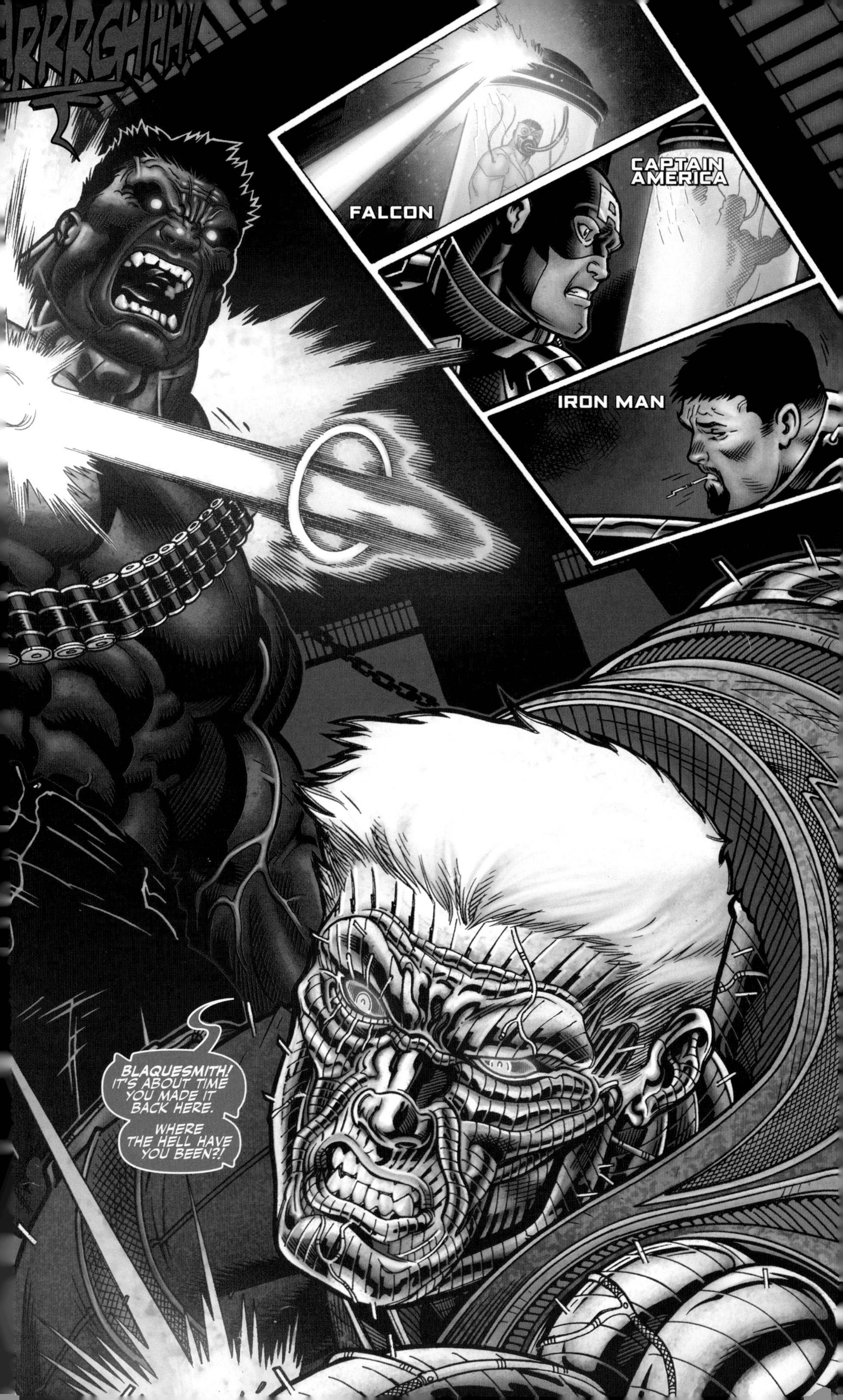
ARRRGHHH!
FALCON
CAPTAIN AMERICA
IRON MAN
BLAQUESMITH! IT'S ABOUT TIME YOU MADE IT BACK HERE.
WHERE THE HELL HAVE YOU BEEN?!

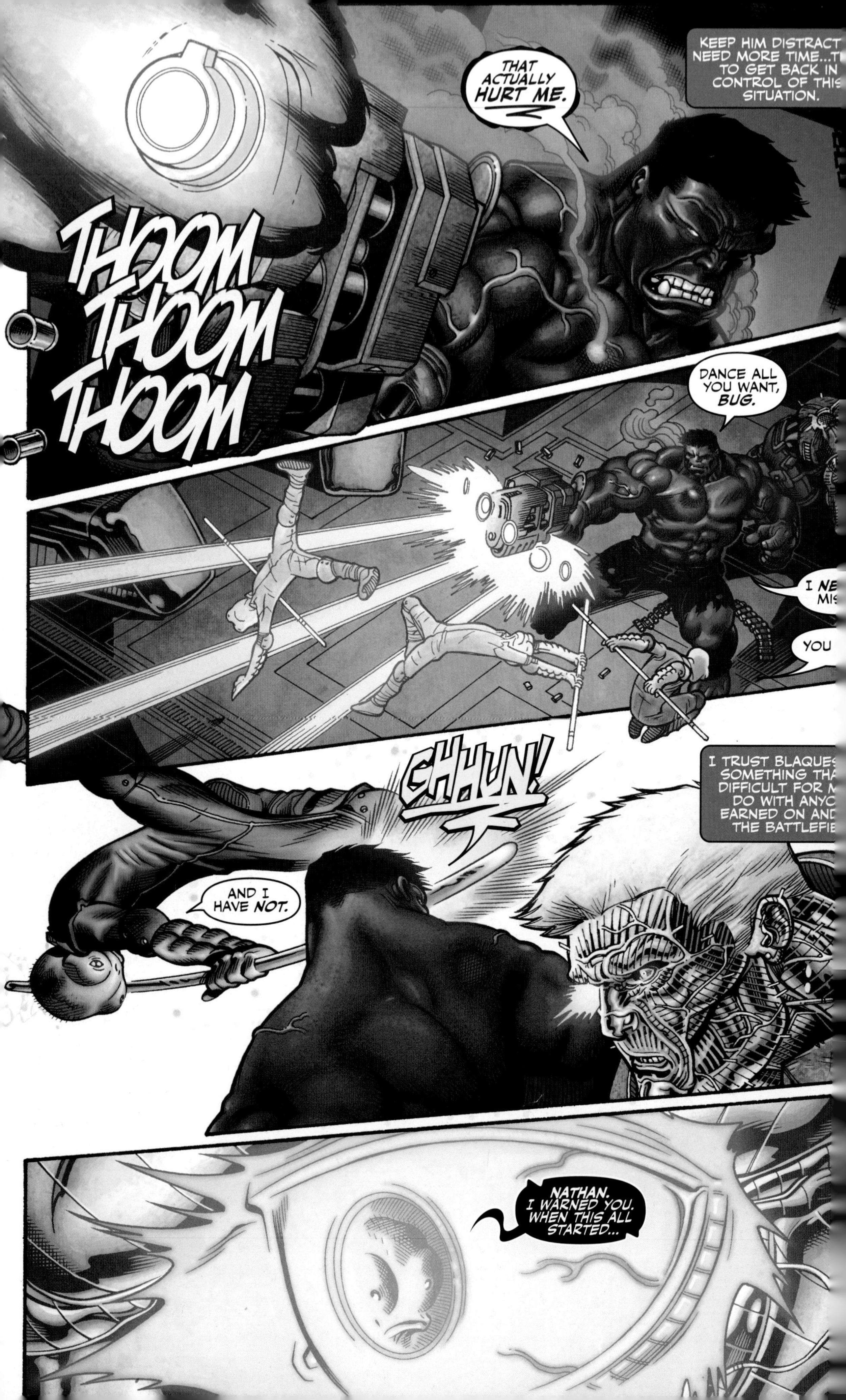

KEEP HIM DISTRACT
NEED MORE TIME...T
TO GET BACK IN
CONTROL OF THIS
SITUATION.
THAT ACTUALLY HURT ME.
THOOM THOOM THOOM
DANCE ALL YOU WANT, BUG.
I NE
MIS
YOU
CHUN!
I TRUST BLAQUES
SOMETHING THA
DIFFICULT FOR M
DO WITH ANYO
EARNED ON AND
THE BATTLEFIE
AND I HAVE NOT.
NATHAN. I WARNED YOU. WHEN THIS ALL STARTED...

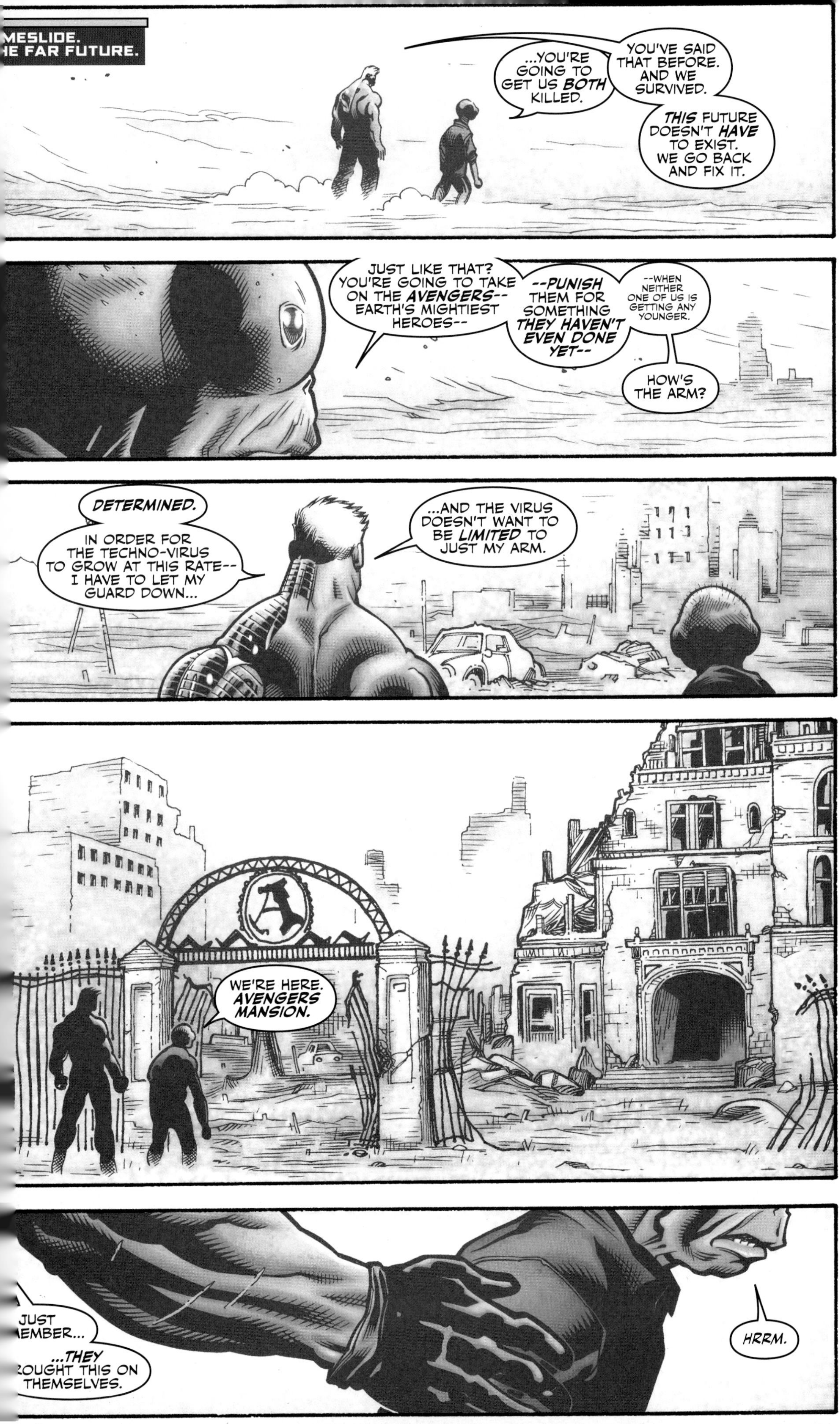

MESLIDE.
HE FAR FUTURE.
...YOU'RE GOING TO GET US BOTH KILLED.
YOU'VE SAID THAT BEFORE. AND WE SURVIVED.
THIS FUTURE DOESN'T HAVE TO EXIST. WE GO BACK AND FIX IT.
JUST LIKE THAT? YOU'RE GOING TO TAKE ON THE AVENGERS-- EARTH'S MIGHTIEST HEROES--
--PUNISH THEM FOR SOMETHING THEY HAVEN'T EVEN DONE YET--
--WHEN NEITHER ONE OF US IS GETTING ANY YOUNGER.
HOW'S THE ARM?
DETERMINED.
IN ORDER FOR THE TECHNO-VIRUS TO GROW AT THIS RATE-- I HAVE TO LET MY GUARD DOWN...
...AND THE VIRUS DOESN'T WANT TO BE LIMITED TO JUST MY ARM.
WE'RE HERE. AVENGERS MANSION.
JUST
EMBER...
...THEY
ROUGHT THIS ON THEMSELVES.
HRRM.

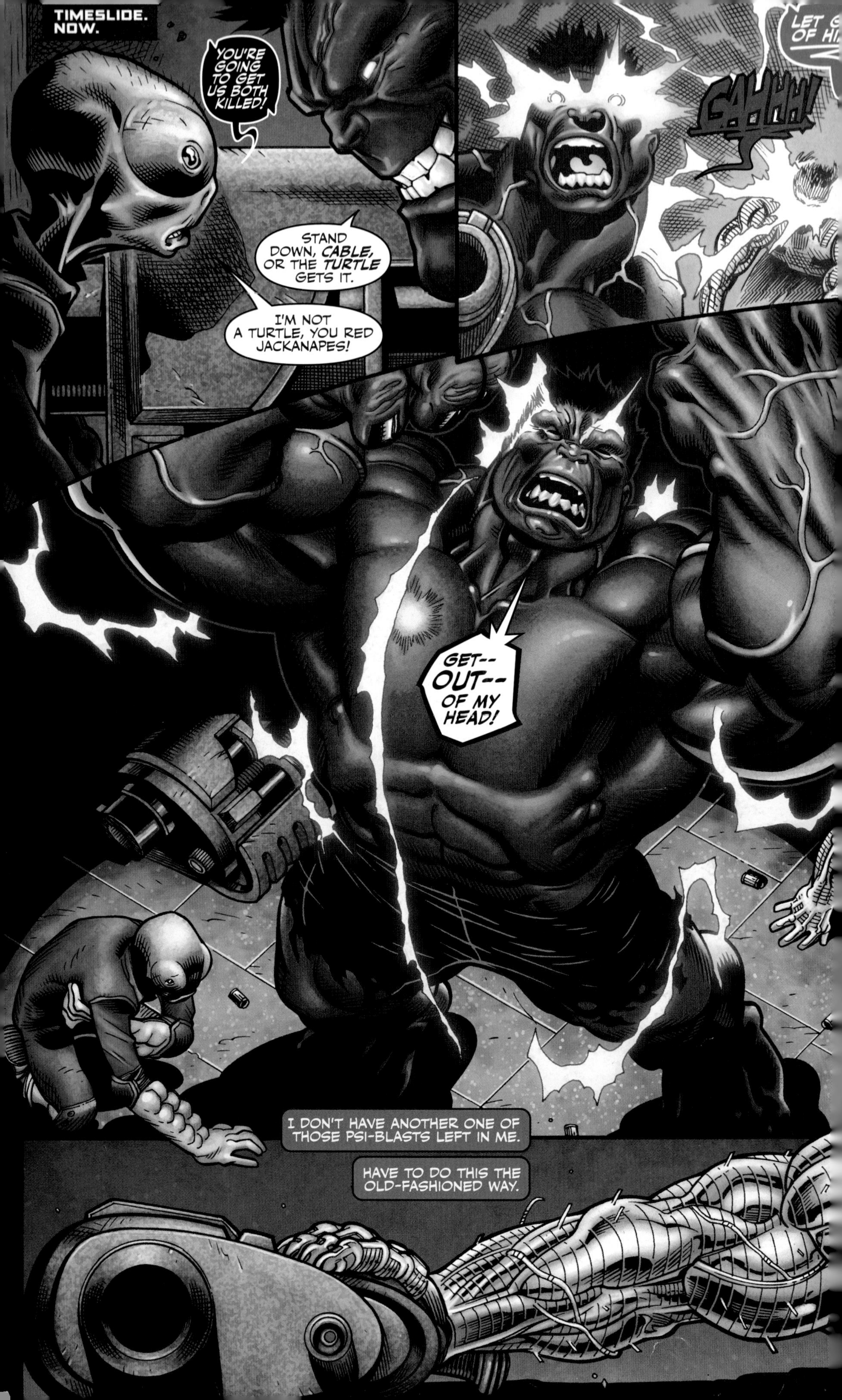
TIMESLIDE. NOW.
YOU'RE GOING TO GET US BOTH KILLED!
STAND DOWN, *CABLE*, OR THE *TURTLE* GETS IT.
I'M NOT A TURTLE, YOU RED JACKANAPES!
GAHHH!
GET-- *OUT*-- OF MY HEAD!
I DON'T HAVE ANOTHER ONE OF THOSE PSI-BLASTS LEFT IN ME.
HAVE TO DO THIS THE OLD-FASHIONED WAY.

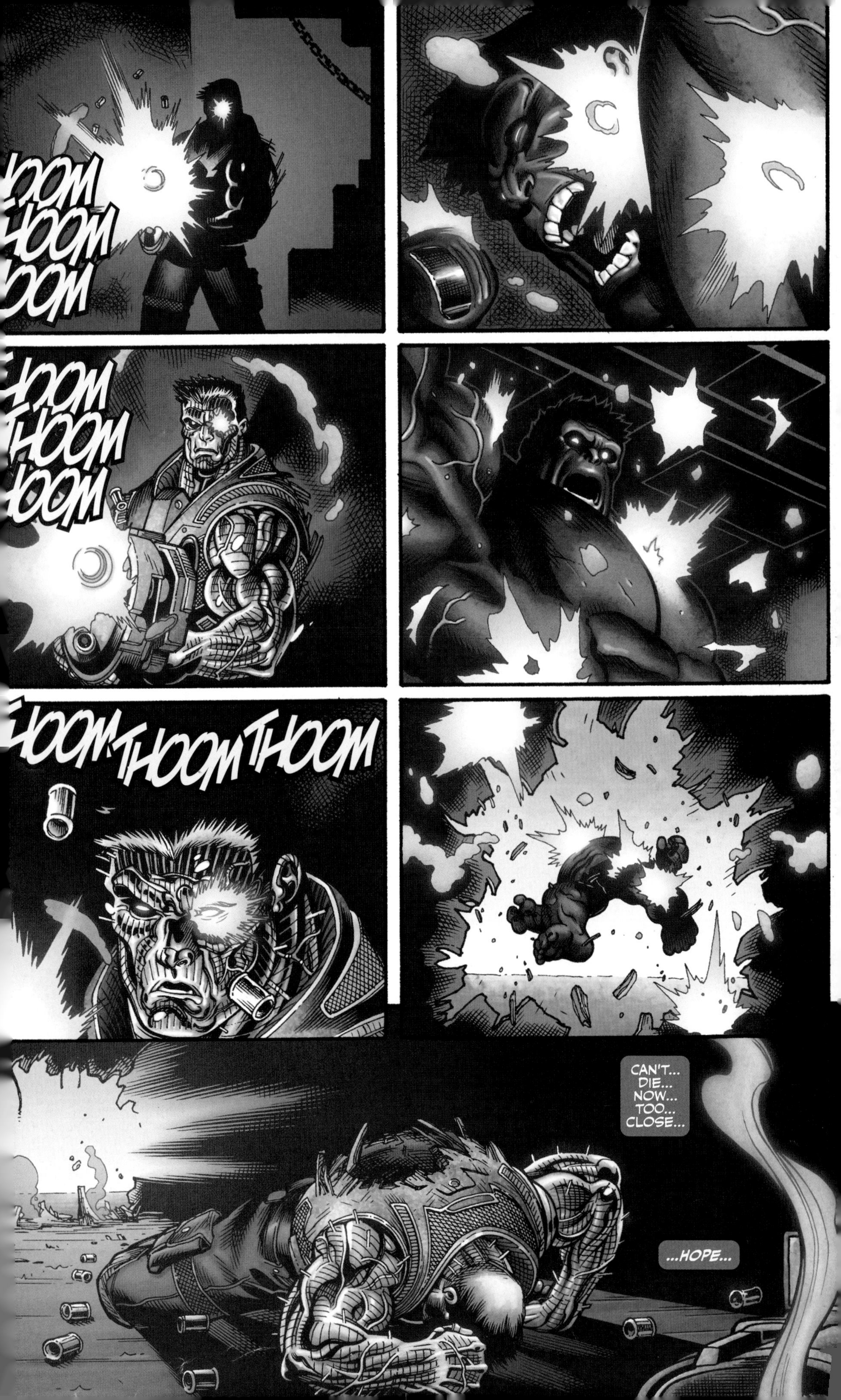
THOOM
THOOM
THOOM
THOOM
THOOM
THOOM
THOOM THOOM THOOM
CAN'T... DIE... NOW... TOO... CLOSE...
...HOPE...

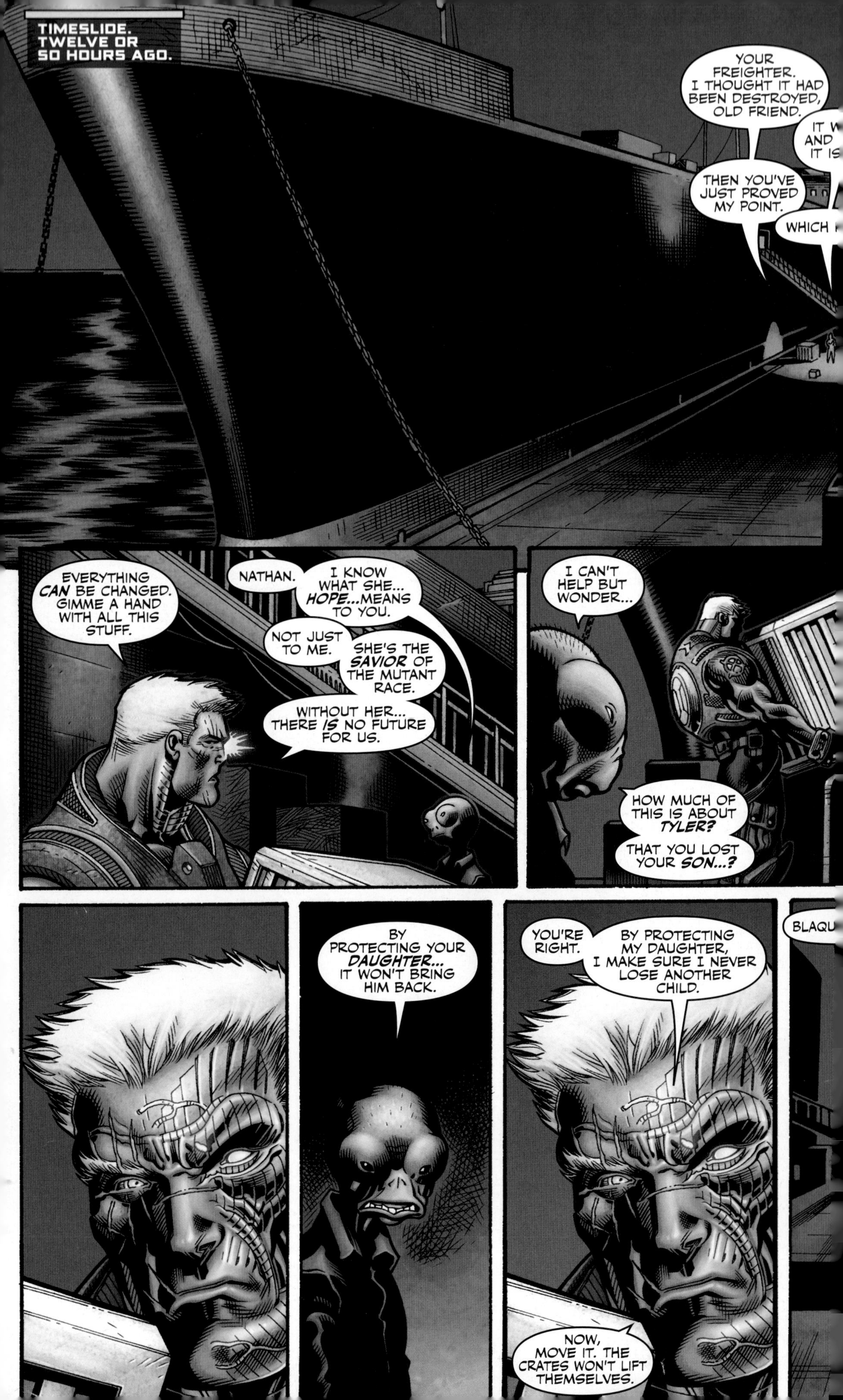
TIMESLIDE. TWELVE OR SO HOURS AGO.
YOUR FREIGHTER. I THOUGHT IT HAD BEEN DESTROYED, OLD FRIEND.
THEN YOU'VE JUST PROVED MY POINT.
EVERYTHING CAN BE CHANGED. GIMME A HAND WITH ALL THIS STUFF.
NATHAN.
I KNOW WHAT SHE... HOPE...MEANS TO YOU.
NOT JUST TO ME.
SHE'S THE SAVIOR OF THE MUTANT RACE.
WITHOUT HER... THERE IS NO FUTURE FOR US.
I CAN'T HELP BUT WONDER...
HOW MUCH OF THIS IS ABOUT TYLER?
THAT YOU LOST YOUR SON...?
BY PROTECTING YOUR DAUGHTER... IT WON'T BRING HIM BACK.
YOU'RE RIGHT.
BY PROTECTING MY DAUGHTER, I MAKE SURE I NEVER LOSE ANOTHER CHILD.
NOW, MOVE IT. THE CRATES WON'T LIFT THEMSELVES.

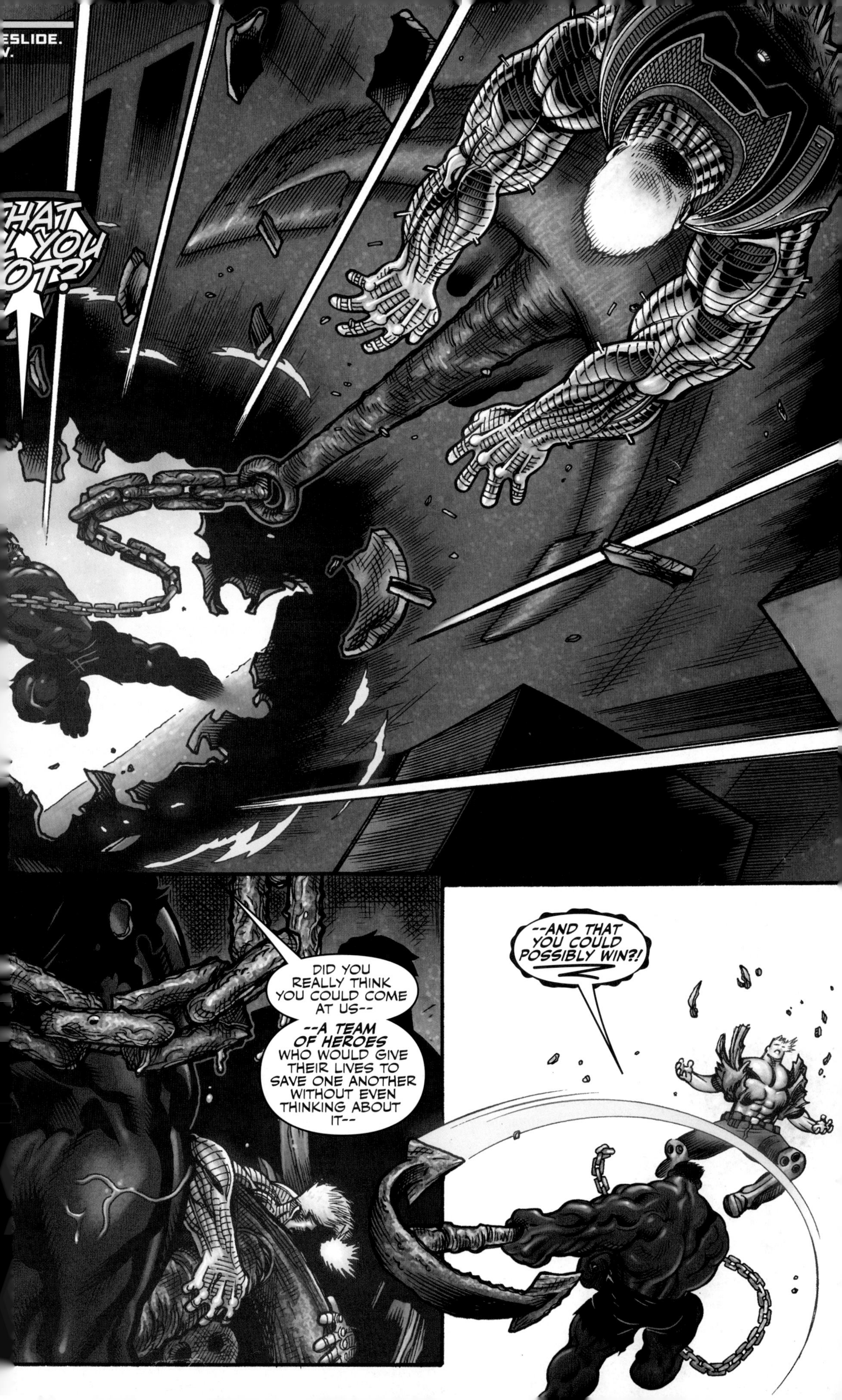
DID YOU REALLY THINK YOU COULD COME AT US--
--A TEAM OF HEROES WHO WOULD GIVE THEIR LIVES TO SAVE ONE ANOTHER WITHOUT EVEN THINKING ABOUT IT--
--AND THAT YOU COULD POSSIBLY WIN?!

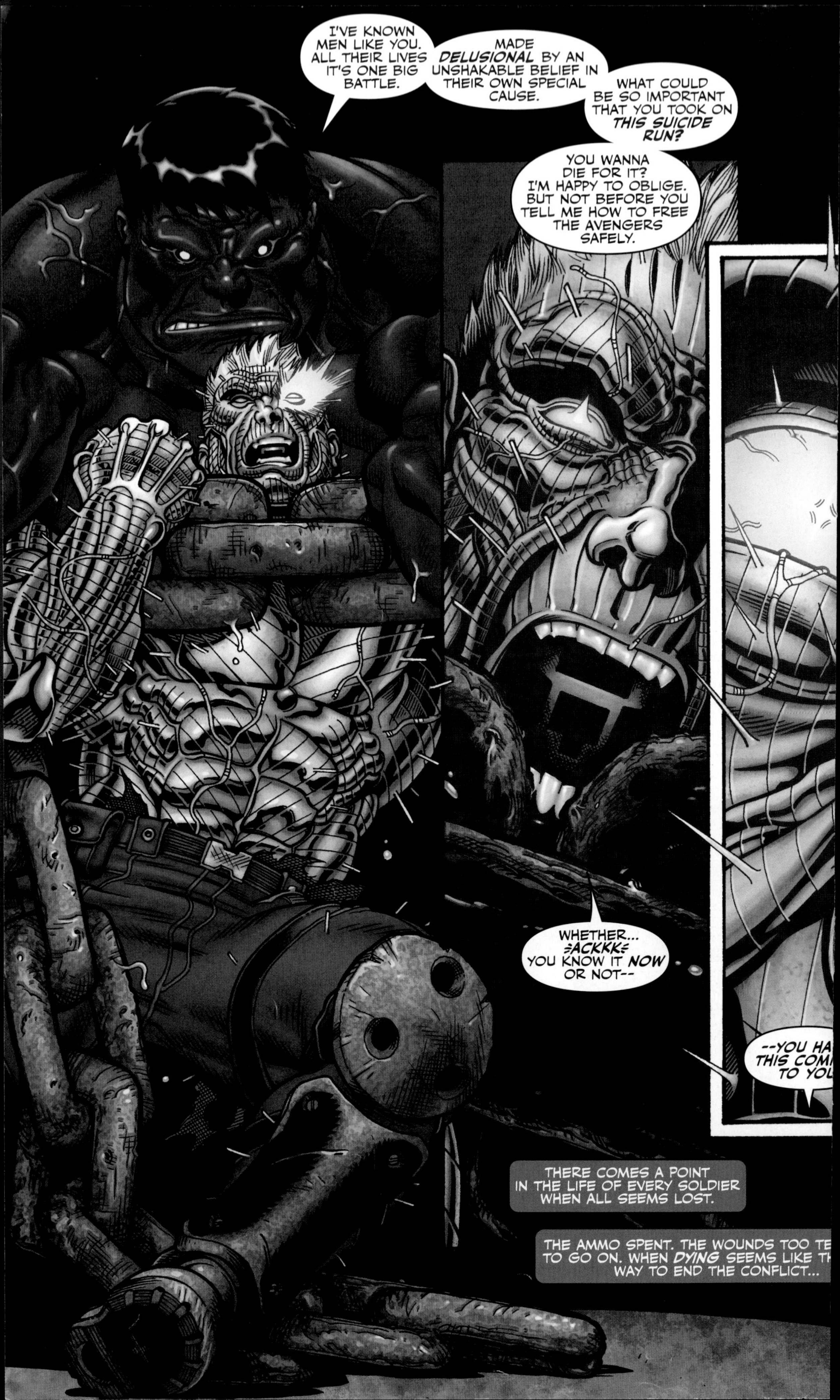
I'VE KNOWN MEN LIKE YOU. ALL THEIR LIVES IT'S ONE BIG BATTLE.
MADE *DELUSIONAL* BY AN UNSHAKABLE BELIEF IN THEIR OWN SPECIAL CAUSE.
WHAT COULD BE SO IMPORTANT THAT YOU TOOK ON *THIS SUICIDE RUN?*
YOU WANNA DIE FOR IT? I'M HAPPY TO OBLIGE. BUT NOT BEFORE YOU TELL ME HOW TO FREE THE AVENGERS SAFELY.
WHETHER... ACKKK YOU KNOW IT *NOW* OR NOT--
THERE COMES A POINT IN THE LIFE OF EVERY SOLDIER WHEN ALL SEEMS LOST.
THE AMMO SPENT. THE WOUNDS TOO TE
TO GO ON. WHEN *DYING* SEEMS LIKE TH
WAY TO END THE CONFLICT...

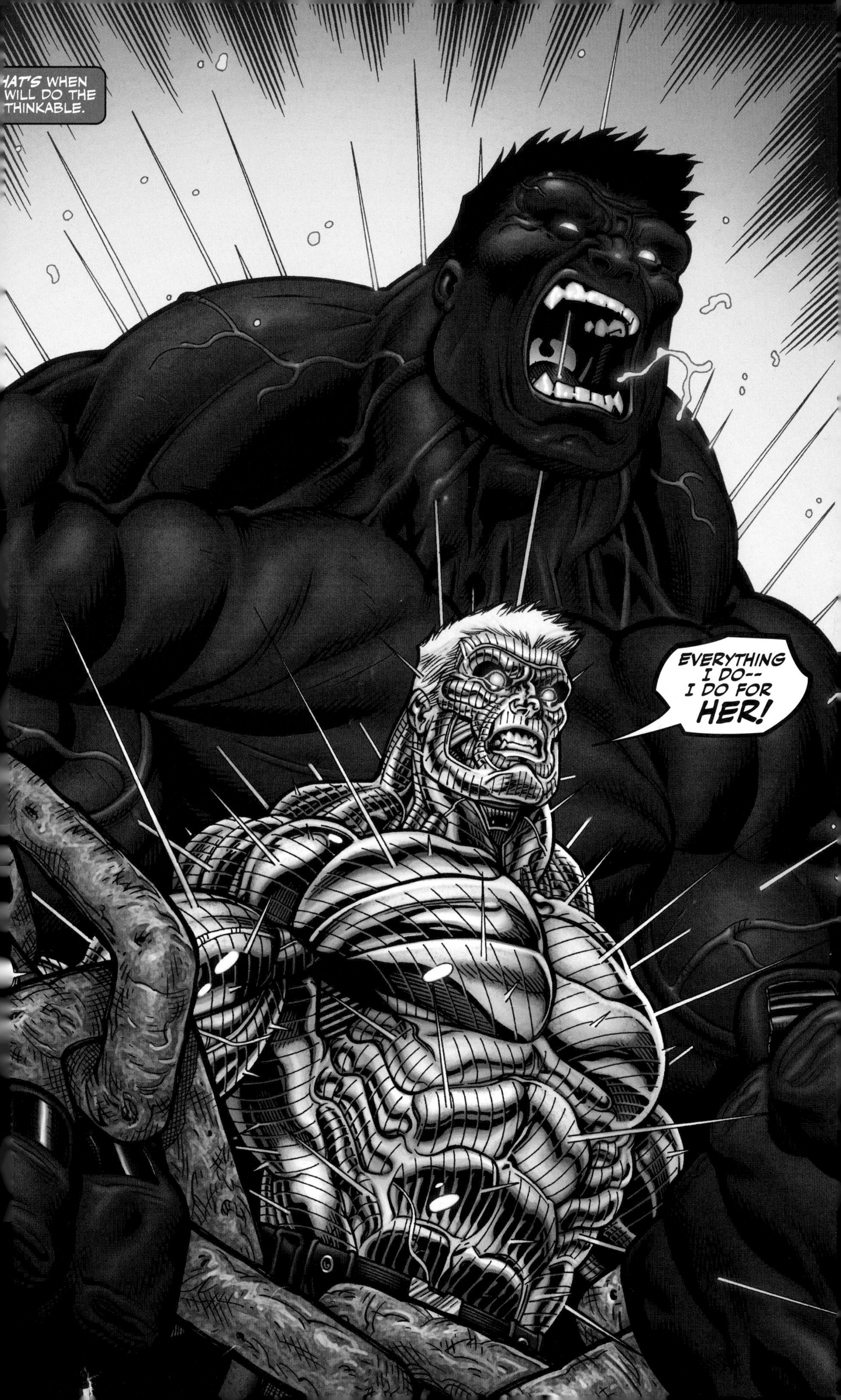
HAT'S WHEN
WILL DO THE
THINKABLE.
EVERYTHING I DO-- I DO FOR HER!

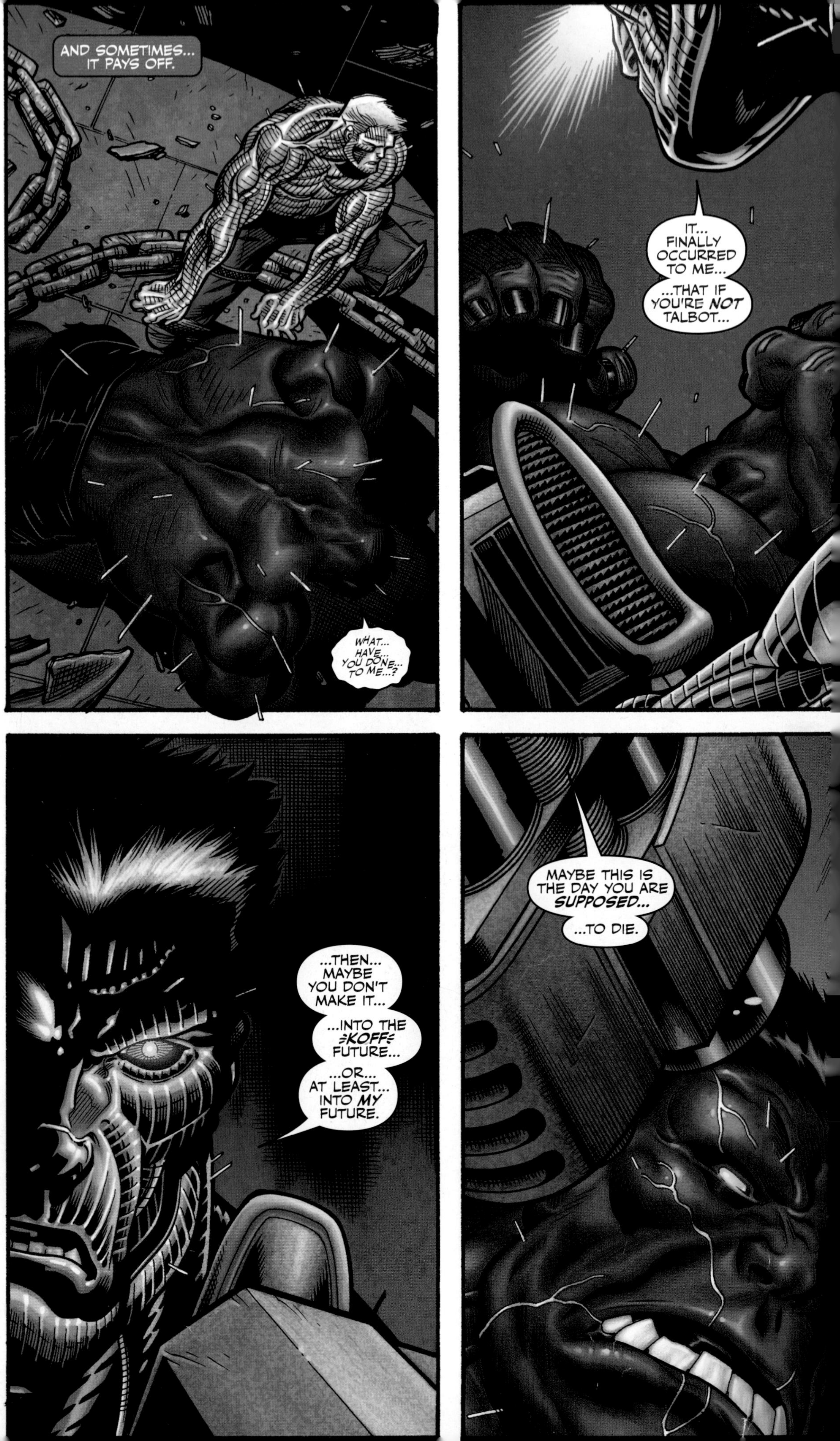
AND SOMETIMES... IT PAYS OFF.
WHAT... HAVE... YOU DONE... TO ME...?
IT... FINALLY OCCURRED TO ME...
...THAT IF YOU'RE NOT TALBOT...
...THEN... MAYBE YOU DON'T MAKE IT...
...INTO THE KOFF FUTURE...
...OR... AT LEAST... INTO MY FUTURE.
MAYBE THIS IS THE DAY YOU ARE SUPPOSED...
...TO DIE.

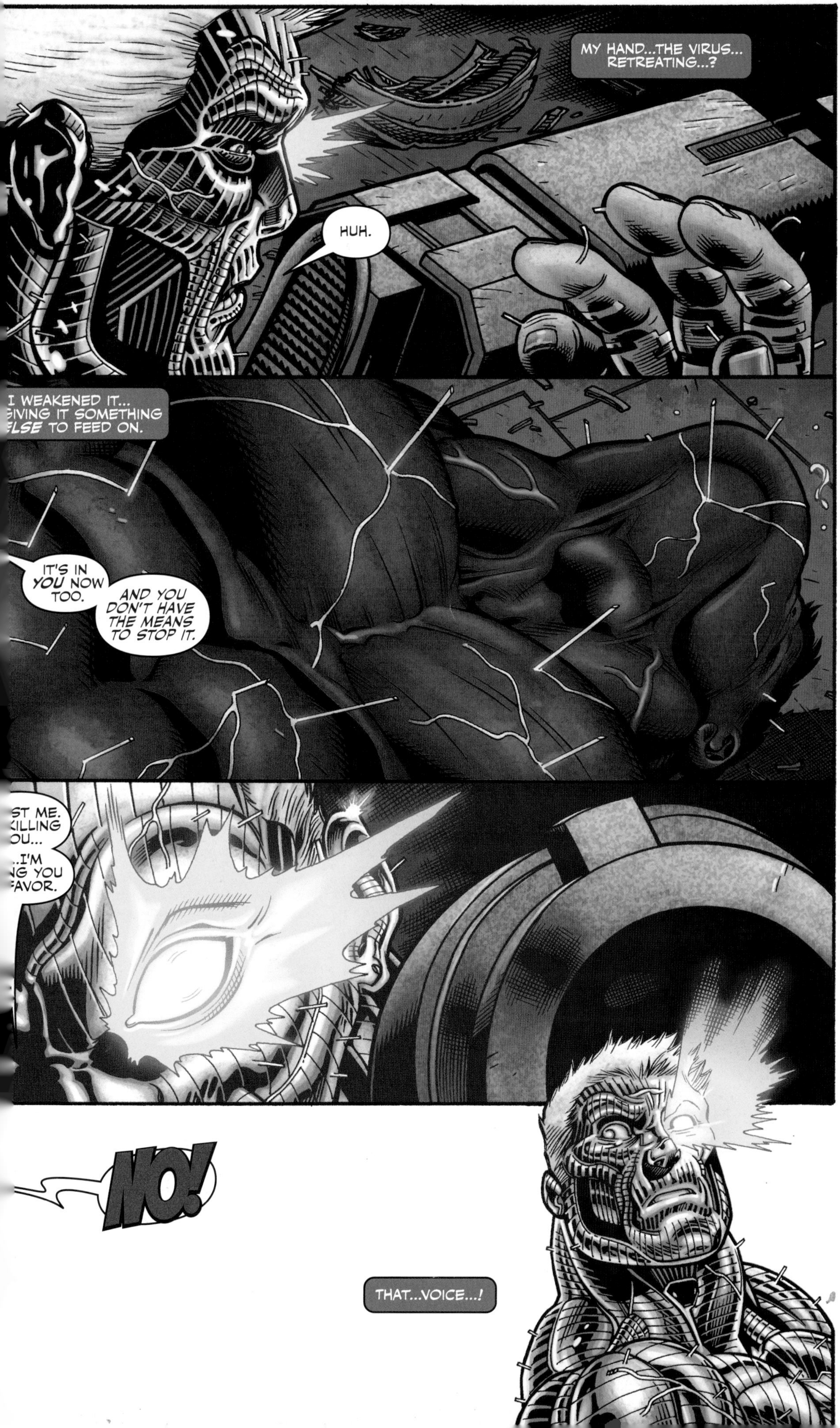
MY HAND...THE VIRUS... RETREATING...?
HUH.
I WEAKENED IT... GIVING IT SOMETHING ELSE TO FEED ON.
IT'S IN YOU NOW TOO.
AND YOU DON'T HAVE THE MEANS TO STOP IT.
NO!
THAT...VOICE...!

MY MIND FLOODS WITH EMOTION. JOY. LOVE. FEAR. ANGER. CONFUSION. *THIS WASN'T PART OF THE PLAN.*

MY DAUGHTER IS HERE. ALONG WITH MY FATHER.

CYCLOPS

HOPE

NATHAN.

DAD. YOU'RE ALIVE!

I NEVER THOUGHT I'D SEE YOU AGAIN.

BLAQUESMITH GOT US.

BLAQUESMITH...? HE *THINKS* HE'S HELPIN' BUT HE'S ONLY PUT HER IN HARM'S WAY.

HE US YOU'V D YOU'VE TO STOP. ALL WR

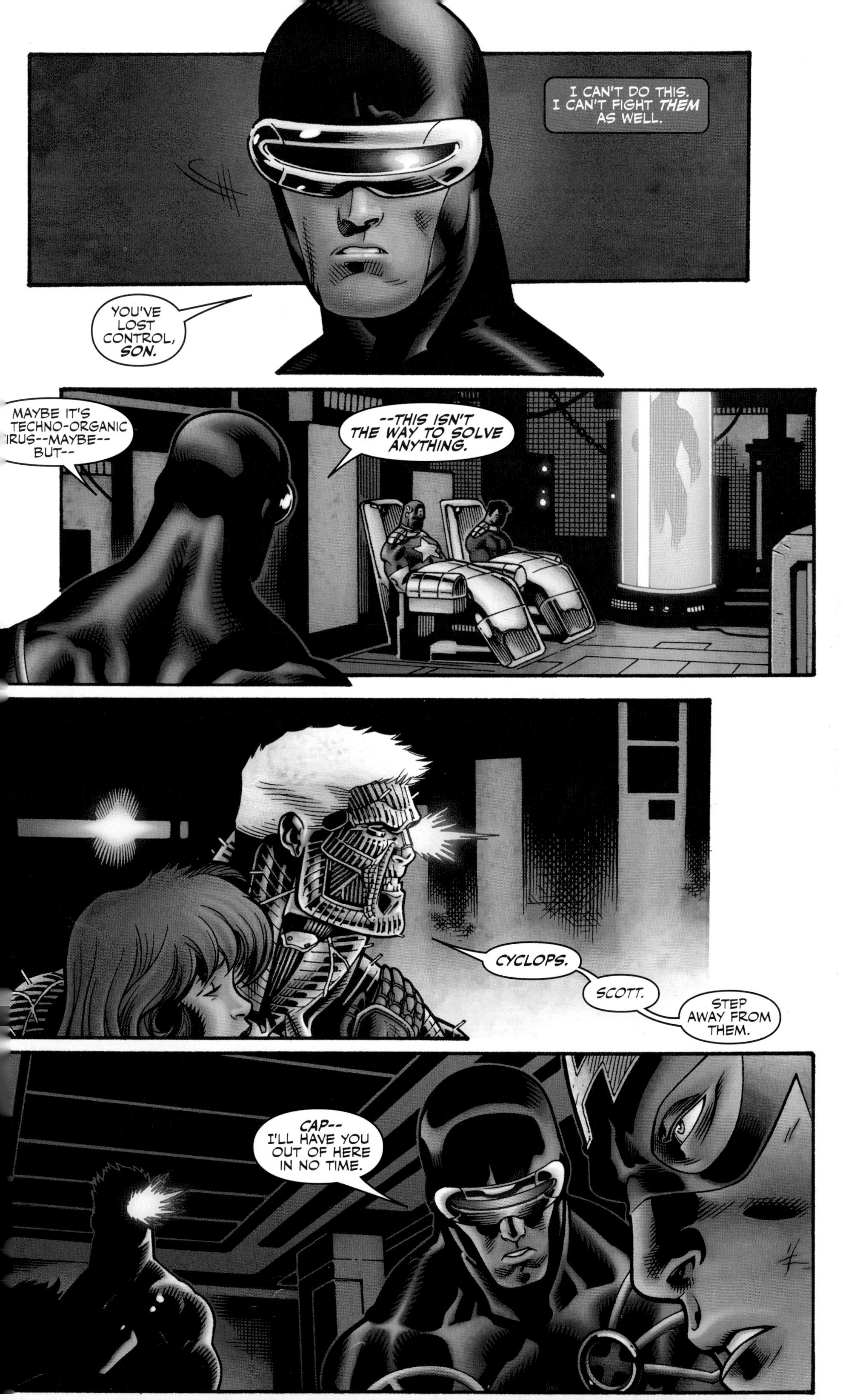
I CAN'T DO THIS. I CAN'T FIGHT *THEM* AS WELL.
YOU'VE LOST CONTROL, *SON.*
MAYBE IT'S TECHNO-ORGANIC IRUS--MAYBE-- BUT--
--THIS ISN'T THE WAY TO SOLVE ANYTHING.
CYCLOPS.
SCOTT.
STEP AWAY FROM THEM.
CAP-- I'LL HAVE YOU OUT OF HERE IN NO TIME.

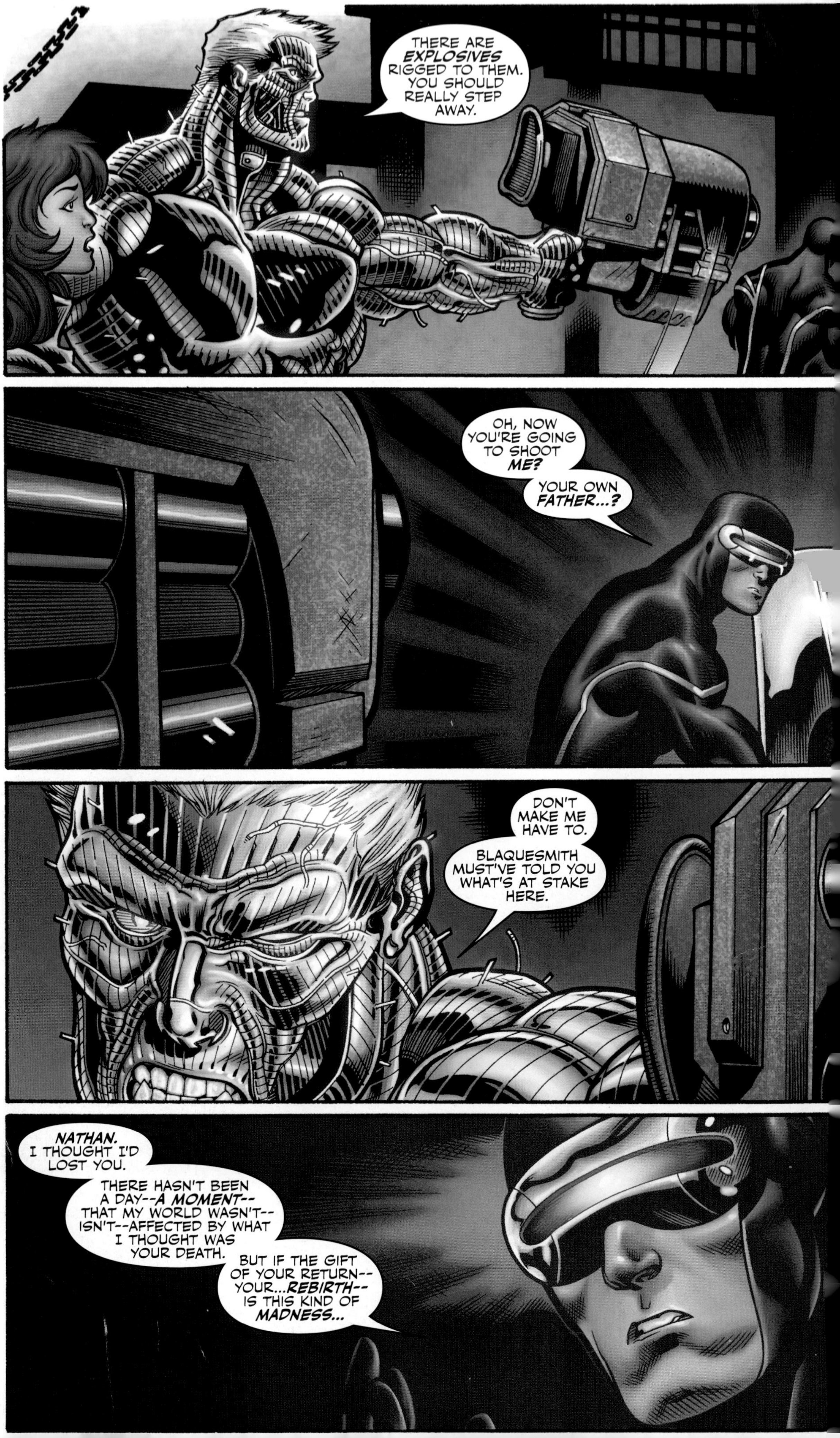
THERE ARE EXPLOSIVES RIGGED TO THEM. YOU SHOULD REALLY STEP AWAY.
OH, NOW YOU'RE GOING TO SHOOT ME?
YOUR OWN FATHER...?
DON'T MAKE ME HAVE TO.
BLAQUESMITH MUST'VE TOLD YOU WHAT'S AT STAKE HERE.
NATHAN. I THOUGHT I'D LOST YOU.
THERE HASN'T BEEN A DAY--A MOMENT--THAT MY WORLD WASN'T--ISN'T--AFFECTED BY WHAT I THOUGHT WAS YOUR DEATH.
BUT IF THE GIFT OF YOUR RETURN--YOUR...REBIRTH--IS THIS KIND OF MADNESS...

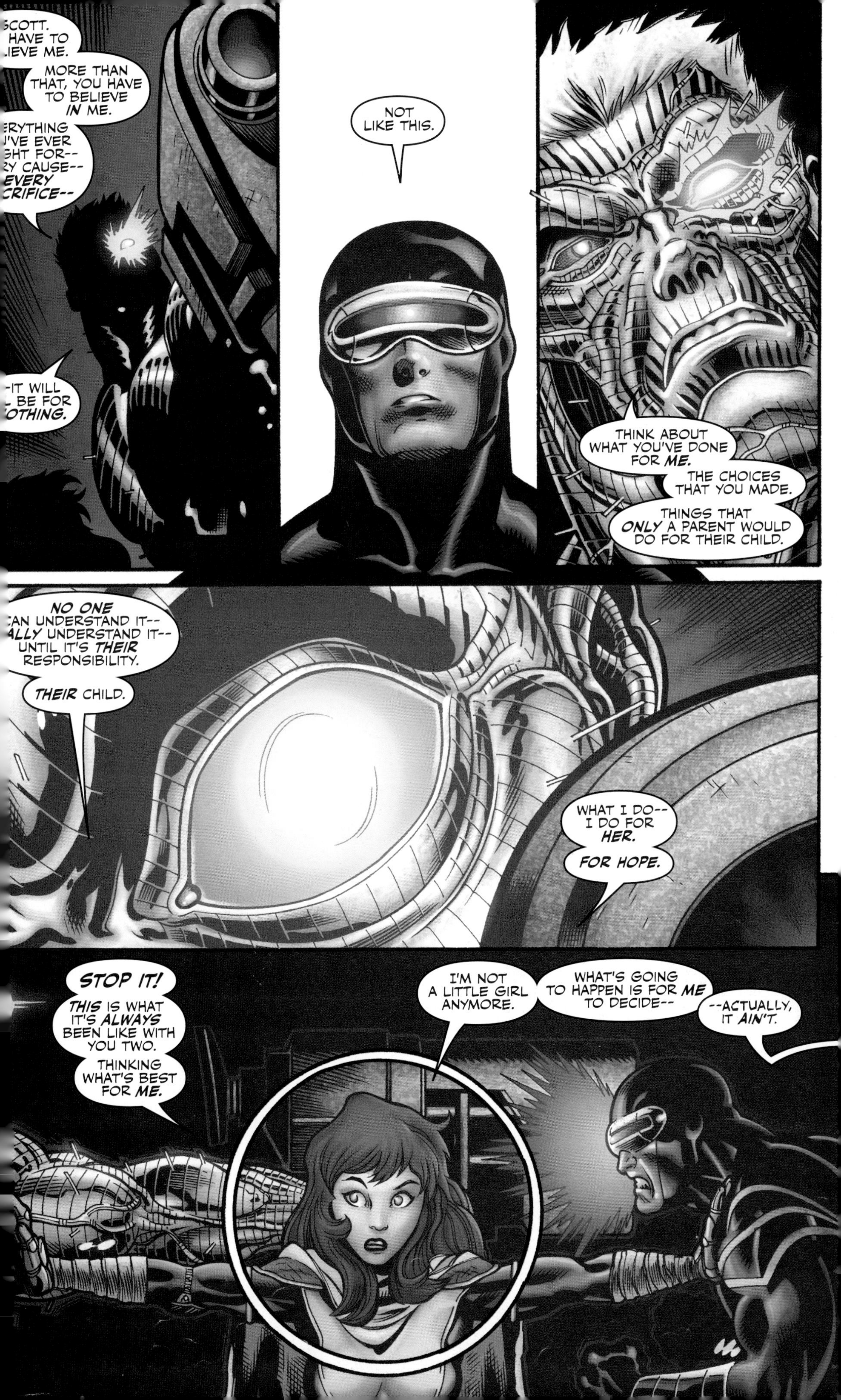

COTT. HAVE TO IEVE ME.
MORE THAN THAT, YOU HAVE TO BELIEVE IN ME.
ERYTHING 'VE EVER GHT FOR-- Y CAUSE-- EVERY CRIFICE--
-IT WILL BE FOR OTHING.
NOT LIKE THIS.
THINK ABOUT WHAT YOU'VE DONE FOR ME.
THE CHOICES THAT YOU MADE.
THINGS THAT ONLY A PARENT WOULD DO FOR THEIR CHILD.
NO ONE CAN UNDERSTAND IT-- ALLY UNDERSTAND IT-- UNTIL IT'S THEIR RESPONSIBILITY.
THEIR CHILD.
WHAT I DO-- I DO FOR HER.
FOR HOPE.
STOP IT!
THIS IS WHAT IT'S ALWAYS BEEN LIKE WITH YOU TWO.
THINKING WHAT'S BEST FOR ME.
I'M NOT A LITTLE GIRL ANYMORE.
WHAT'S GOING TO HAPPEN IS FOR ME TO DECIDE--
--ACTUALLY, IT AIN'T.

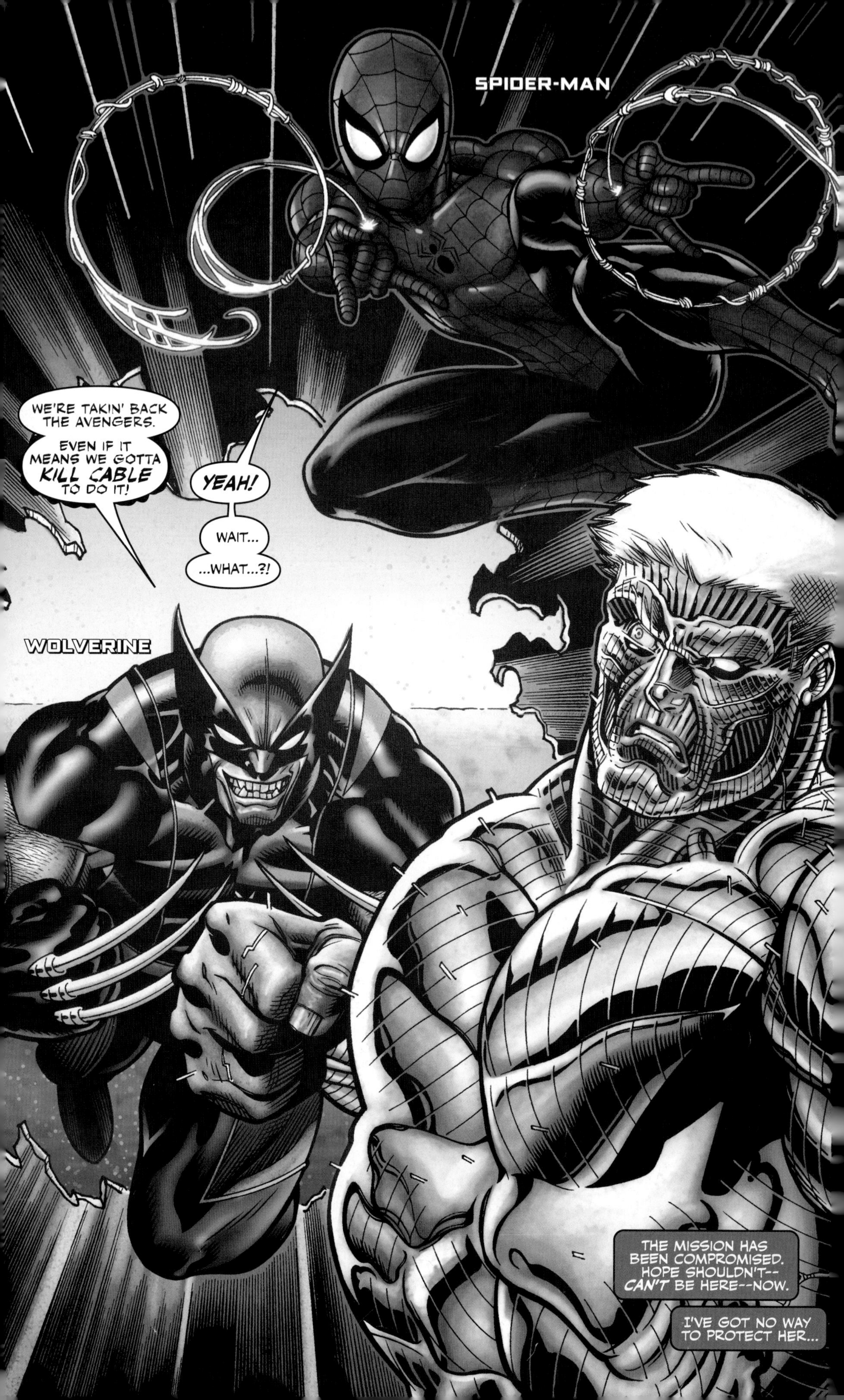
SPIDER-MAN
WE'RE TAKIN' BACK THE AVENGERS.
EVEN IF IT MEANS WE GOTTA KILL CABLE TO DO IT!
YEAH!
WAIT...
...WHAT...?!
WOLVERINE
THE MISSION HAS BEEN COMPROMISED. HOPE SHOULDN'T-- CAN'T BE HERE--NOW.
I'VE GOT NO WAY TO PROTECT HER...

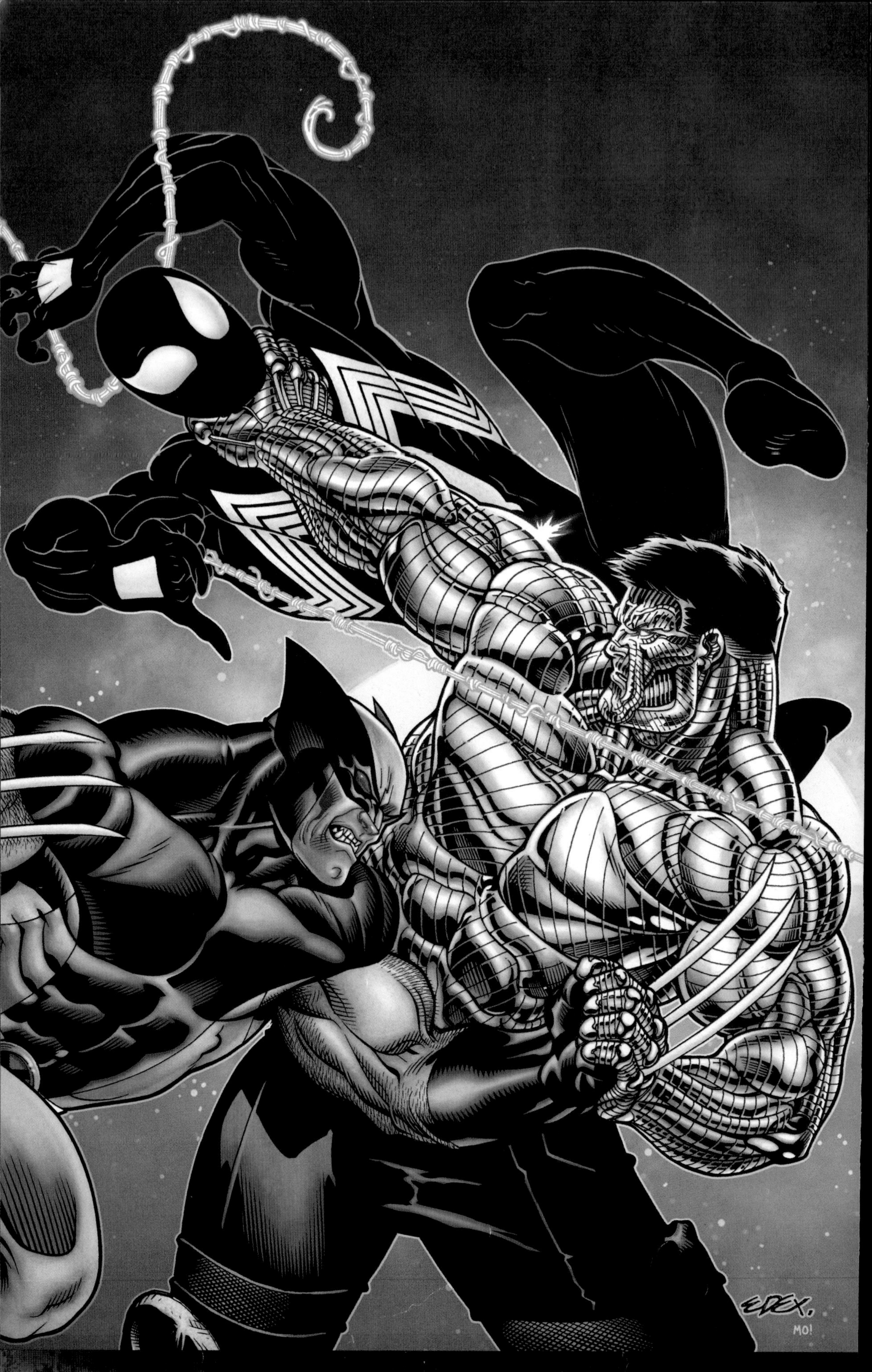

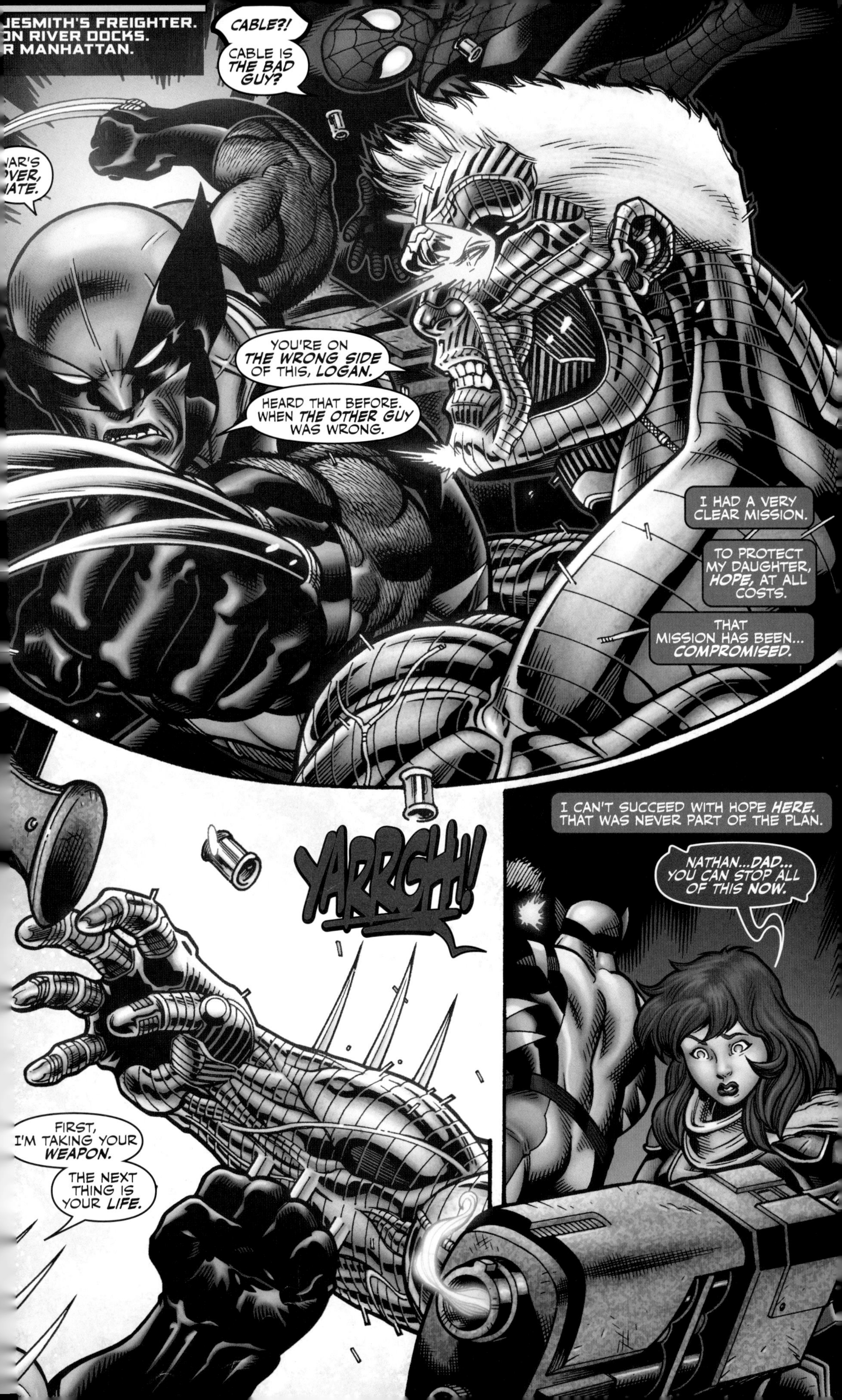

JESMITH'S FREIGHTER.
ON RIVER DOCKS.
R MANHATTAN.
CABLE?!
CABLE IS THE BAD GUY?
WAR'S OVER, MATE.
YOU'RE ON THE WRONG SIDE OF THIS, LOGAN.
HEARD THAT BEFORE. WHEN THE OTHER GUY WAS WRONG.
I HAD A VERY CLEAR MISSION.
TO PROTECT MY DAUGHTER, HOPE, AT ALL COSTS.
THAT MISSION HAS BEEN... COMPROMISED.
YARRGH!
FIRST, I'M TAKING YOUR WEAPON.
THE NEXT THING IS YOUR LIFE.
I CAN'T SUCCEED WITH HOPE HERE. THAT WAS NEVER PART OF THE PLAN.
NATHAN...DAD... YOU CAN STOP ALL OF THIS NOW.

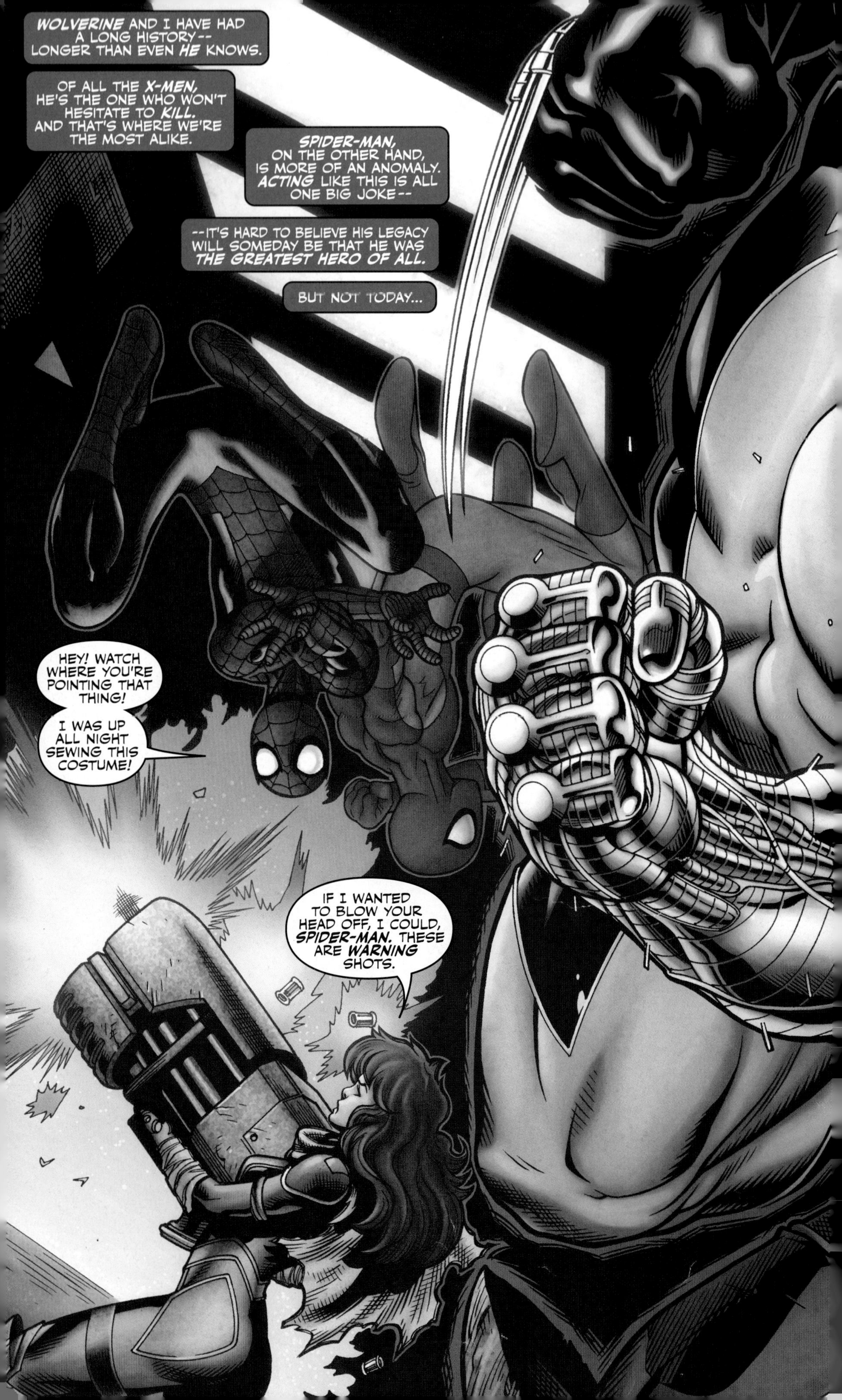

WOLVERINE AND I HAVE HAD A LONG HISTORY-- LONGER THAN EVEN HE KNOWS.
OF ALL THE X-MEN, HE'S THE ONE WHO WON'T HESITATE TO KILL. AND THAT'S WHERE WE'RE THE MOST ALIKE.
SPIDER-MAN, ON THE OTHER HAND, IS MORE OF AN ANOMALY. ACTING LIKE THIS IS ALL ONE BIG JOKE--
--IT'S HARD TO BELIEVE HIS LEGACY WILL SOMEDAY BE THAT HE WAS THE GREATEST HERO OF ALL.
BUT NOT TODAY...
HEY! WATCH WHERE YOU'RE POINTING THAT THING!
I WAS UP ALL NIGHT SEWING THIS COSTUME!
IF I WANTED TO BLOW YOUR HEAD OFF, I COULD, SPIDER-MAN. THESE ARE WARNING SHOTS.

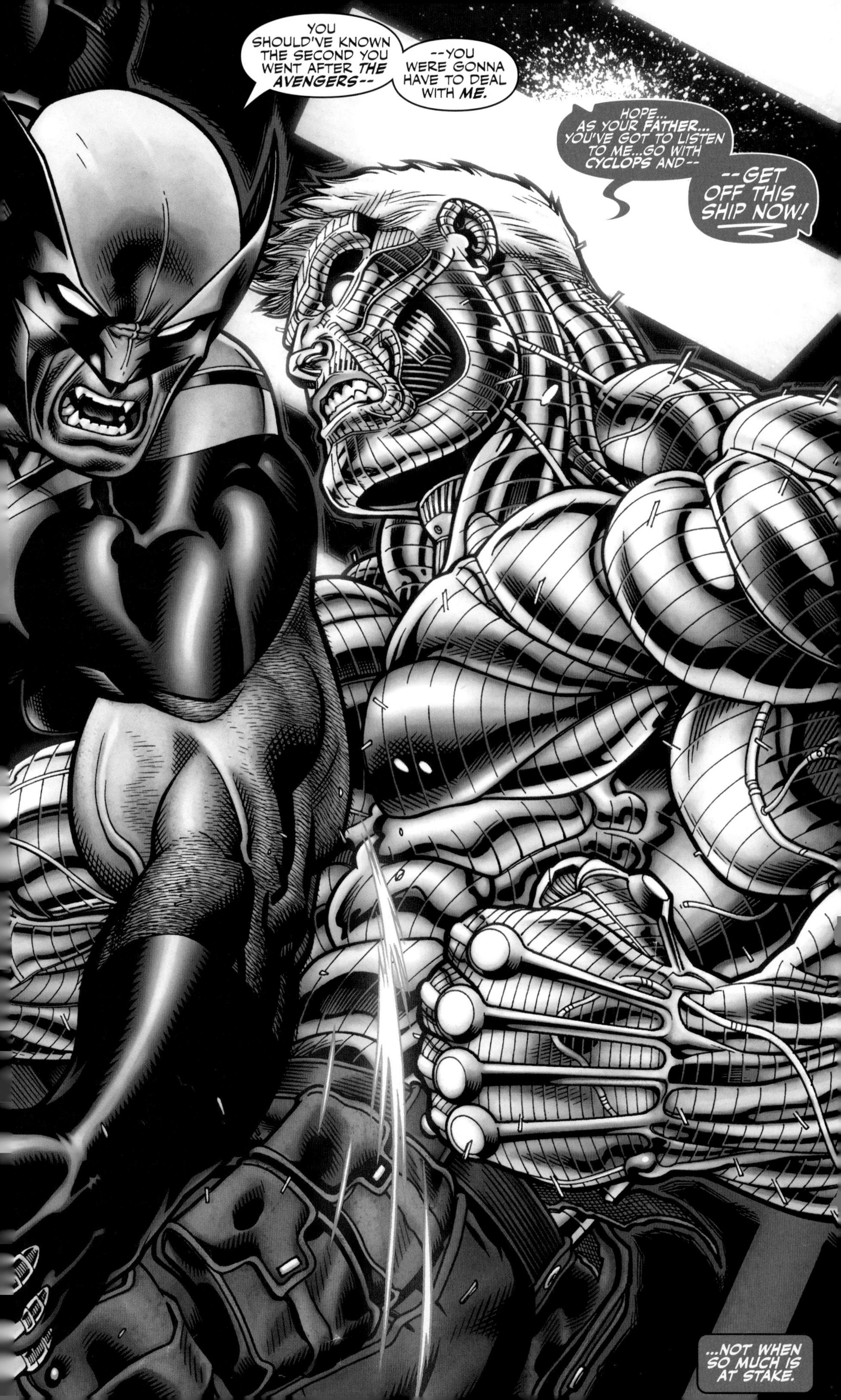

YOU SHOULD'VE KNOWN THE SECOND YOU WENT AFTER *THE AVENGERS*--
--YOU WERE GONNA HAVE TO DEAL WITH *ME.*
HOPE... AS YOUR *FATHER*... YOU'VE GOT TO LISTEN TO ME...GO WITH CYCLOPS AND--
--GET OFF THIS SHIP NOW!
...NOT WHEN SO MUCH IS AT STAKE.

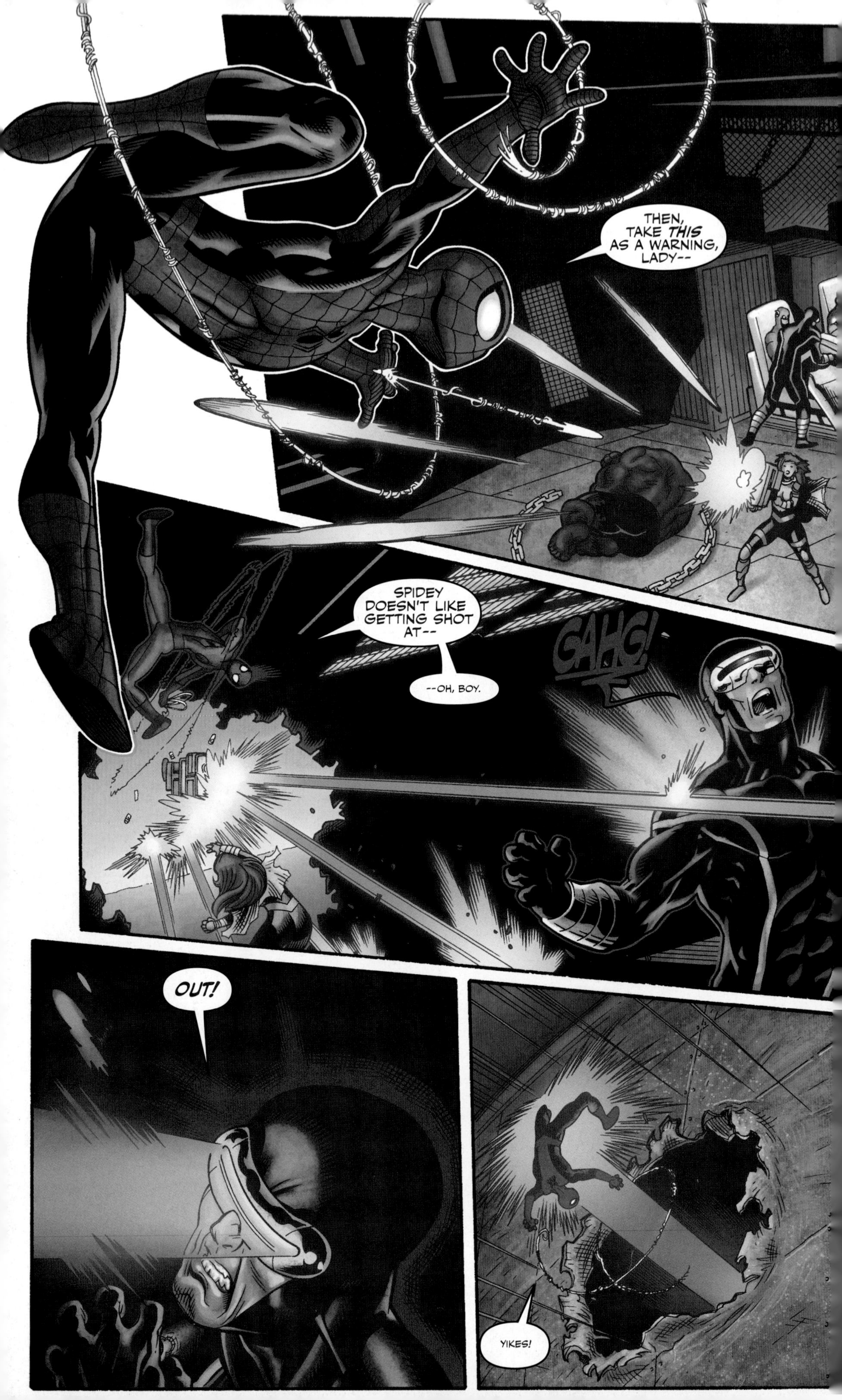
THEN, TAKE *THIS* AS A WARNING, LADY--
SPIDEY DOESN'T LIKE GETTING SHOT AT--
--OH, BOY.
GAHG!
OUT!
YIKES!

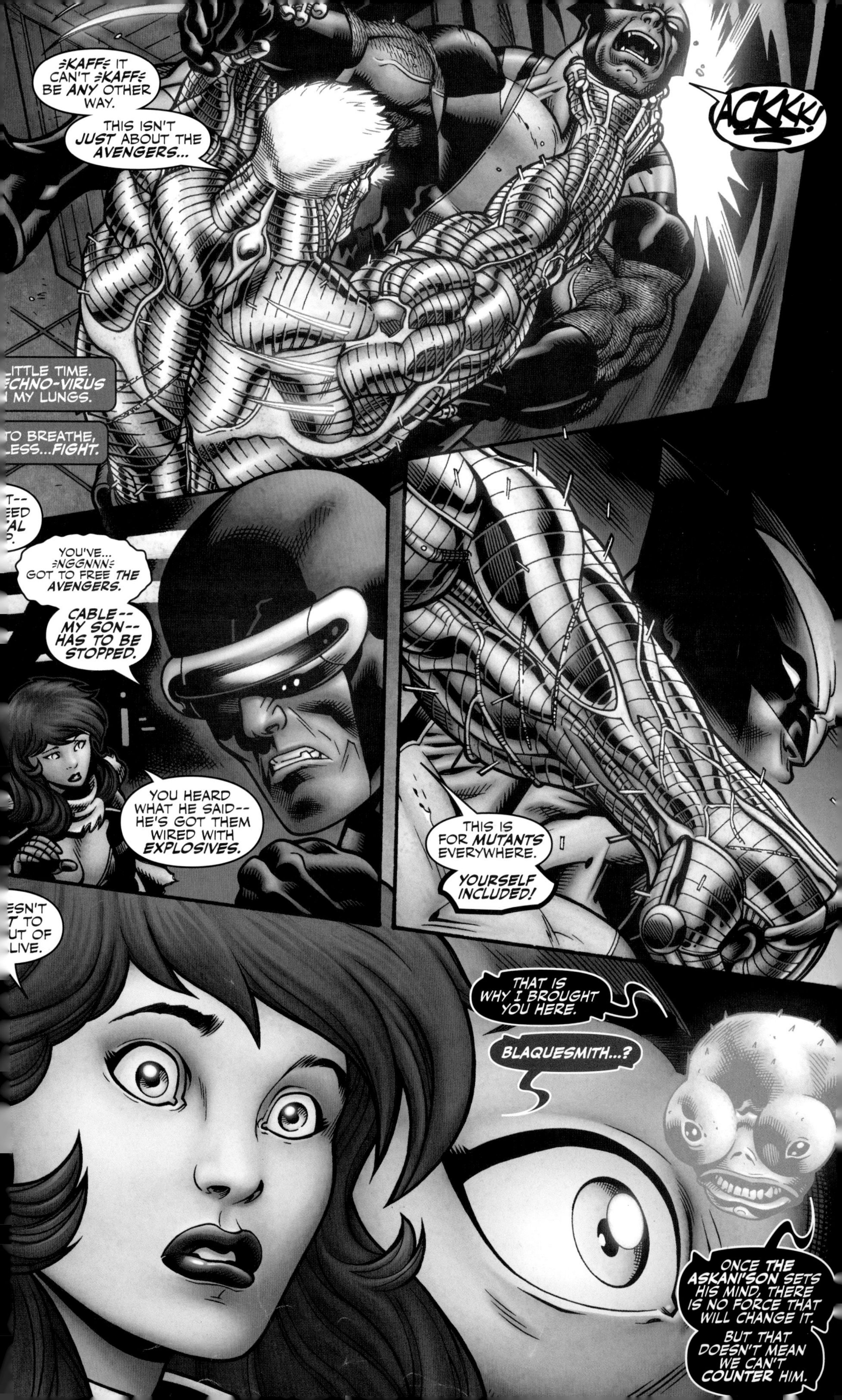

KAFF IT CAN'T KAFF BE ANY OTHER WAY.
THIS ISN'T JUST ABOUT THE AVENGERS...
ACKKK!
YOU'VE... NGGNNN GOT TO FREE THE AVENGERS.
CABLE-- MY SON-- HAS TO BE STOPPED.
YOU HEARD WHAT HE SAID-- HE'S GOT THEM WIRED WITH EXPLOSIVES.
THIS IS FOR MUTANTS EVERYWHERE.
YOURSELF INCLUDED!
THAT IS WHY I BROUGHT YOU HERE.
BLAQUESMITH...?
ONCE THE ASKANI'SON SETS HIS MIND, THERE IS NO FORCE THAT WILL CHANGE IT.
BUT THAT DOESN'T MEAN WE CAN'T COUNTER HIM.

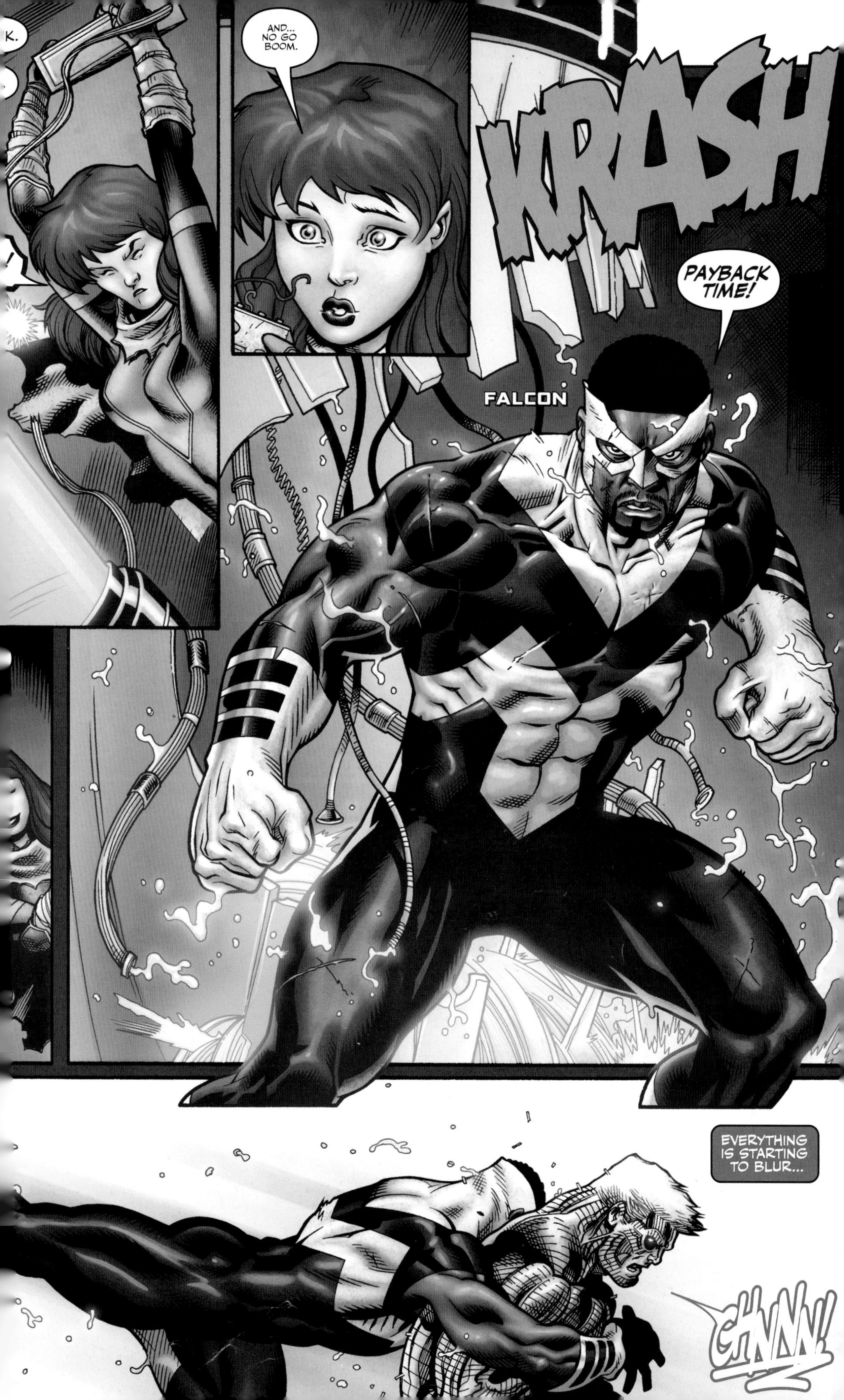
K.
AND... NO GO BOOM.
KRASH
PAYBACK TIME!
FALCON
EVERYTHING IS STARTING TO BLUR...
CHNNN!

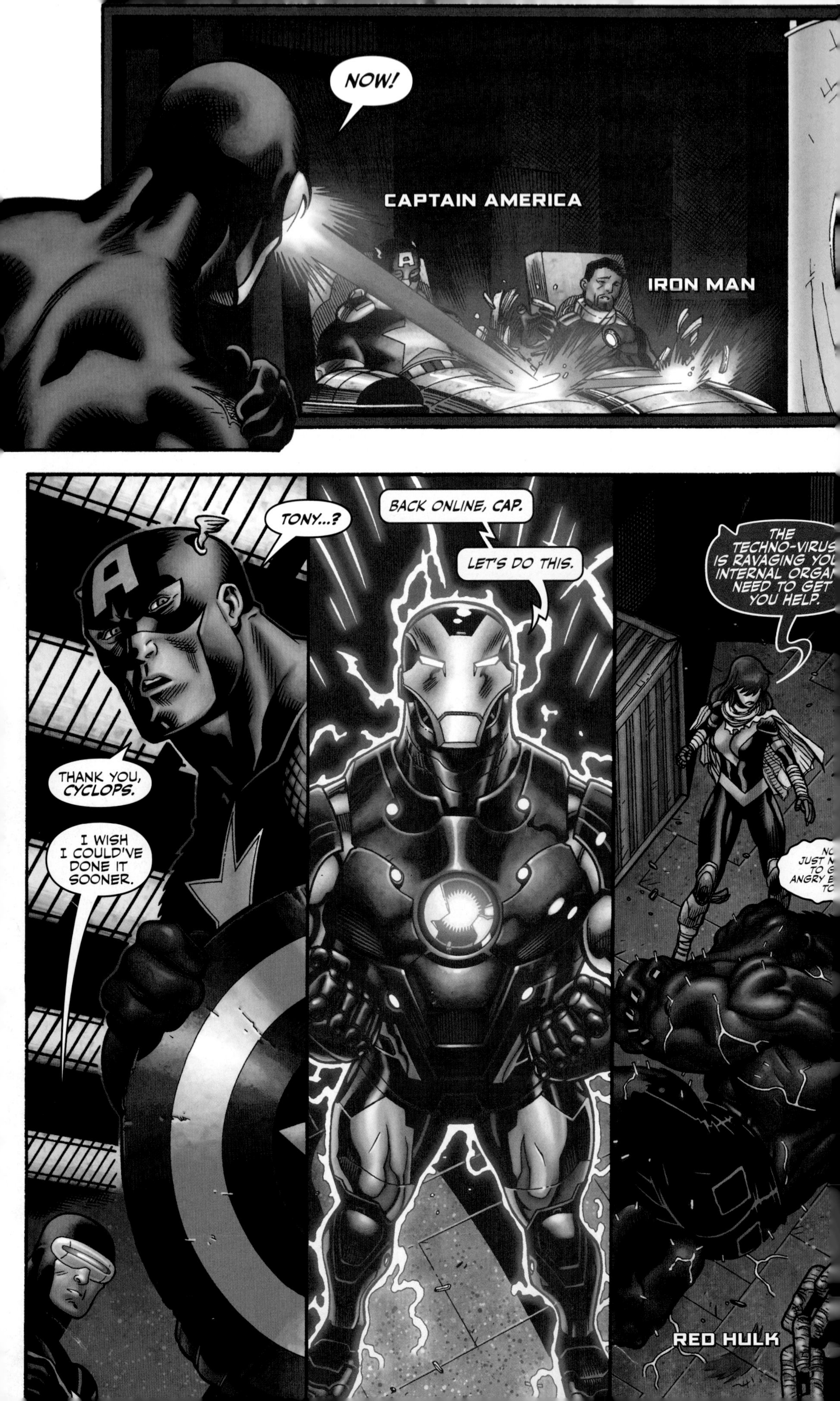
NOW!
CAPTAIN AMERICA
IRON MAN
TONY...?
BACK ONLINE, CAP.
LET'S DO THIS.
THE TECHNO-VIRUS IS RAVAGING YOU INTERNAL ORGA NEED TO GET YOU HELP.
THANK YOU, CYCLOPS.
I WISH I COULD'VE DONE IT SOONER.
RED HULK

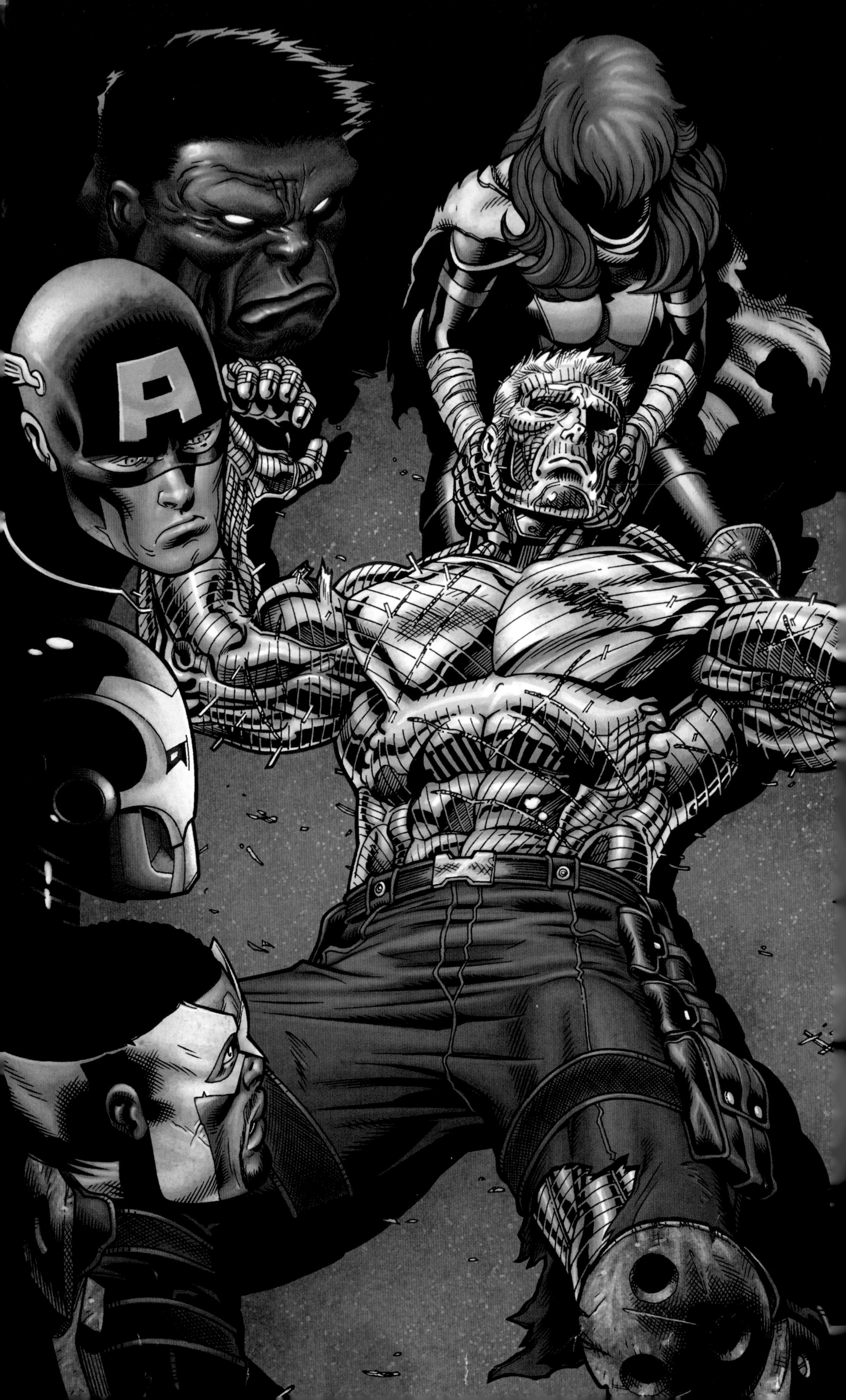

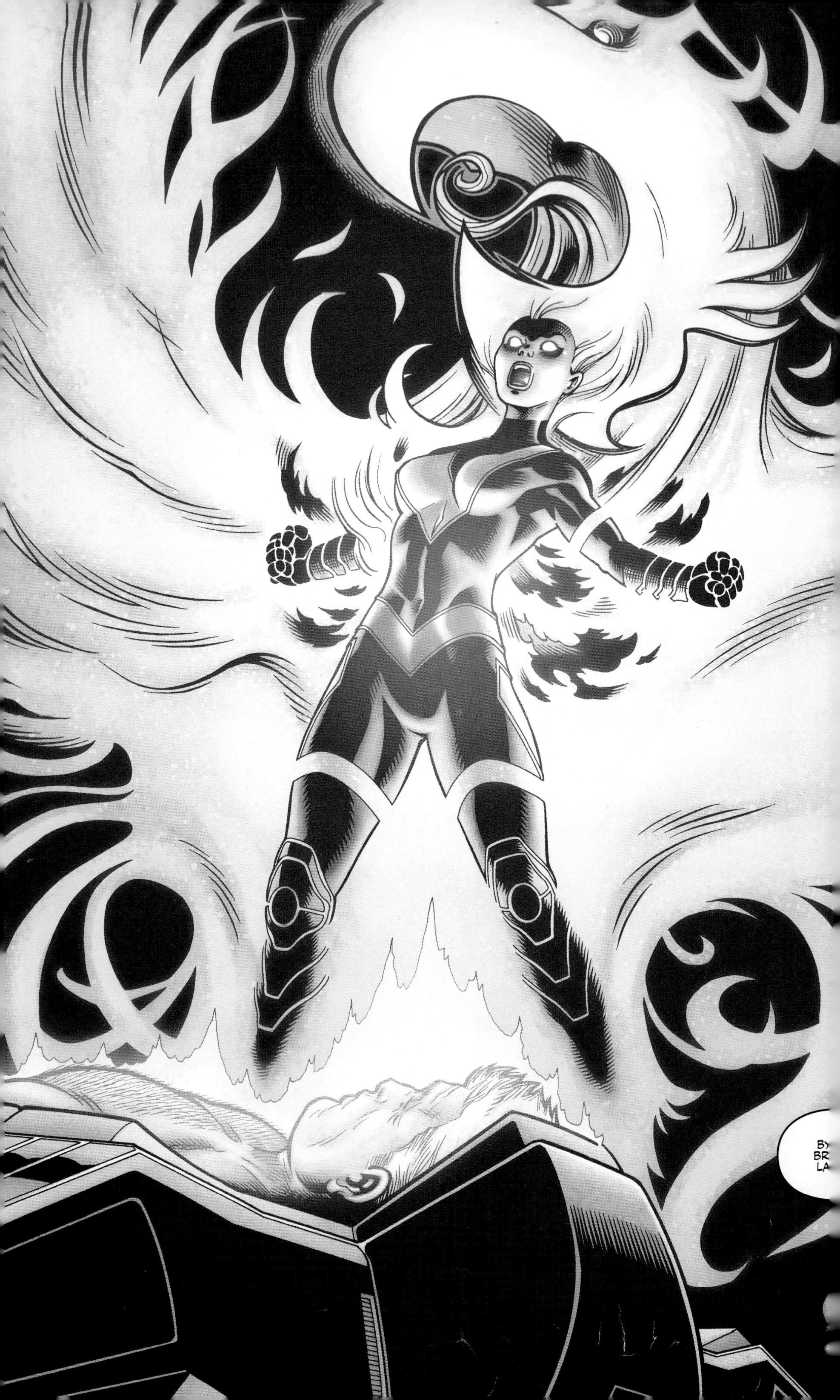

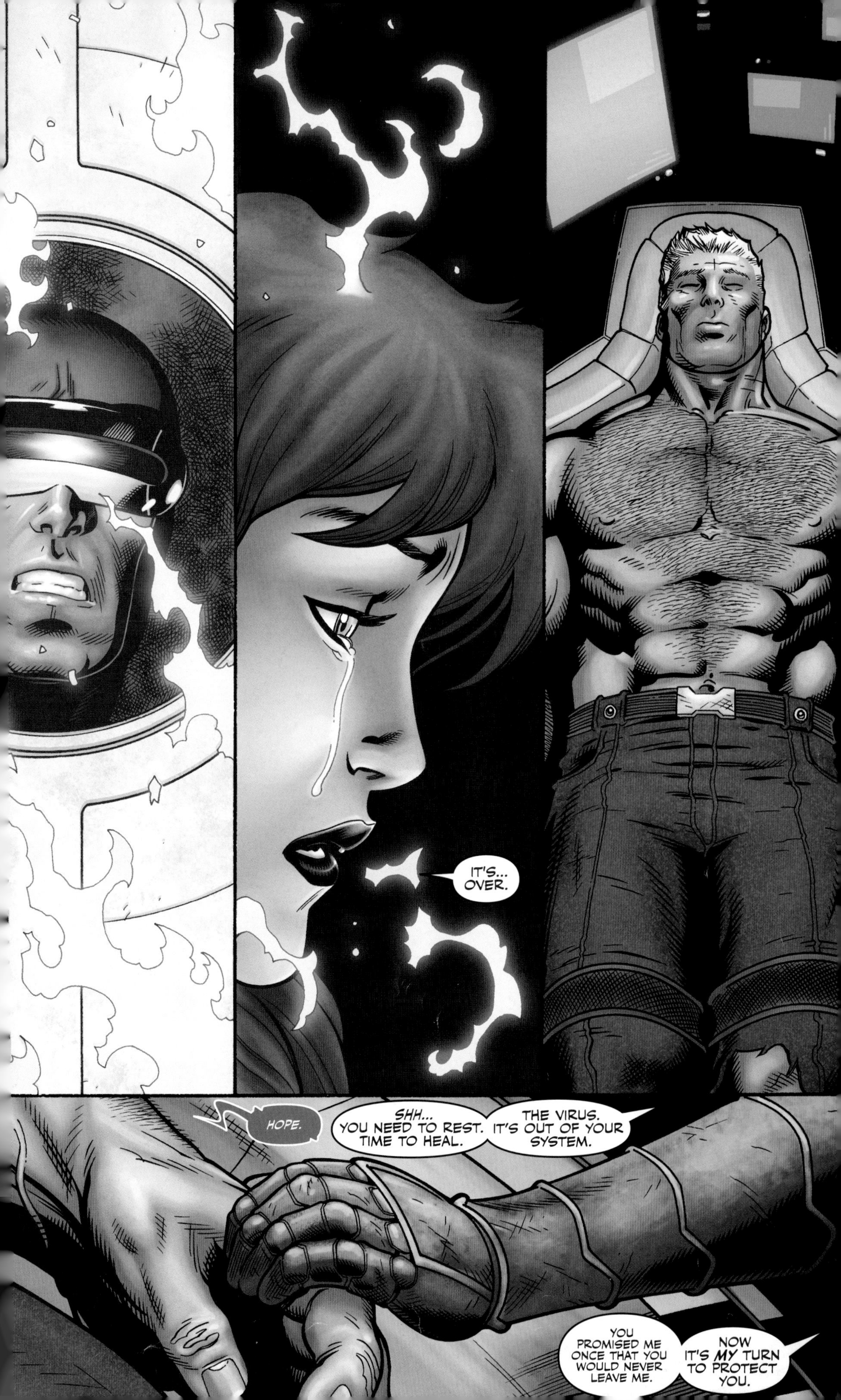
IT'S... OVER.
HOPE.
SHH... YOU NEED TO REST. TIME TO HEAL.
THE VIRUS. IT'S OUT OF YOUR SYSTEM.
YOU PROMISED ME ONCE THAT YOU WOULD NEVER LEAVE ME.
NOW IT'S MY TURN TO PROTECT YOU.

GALLERY

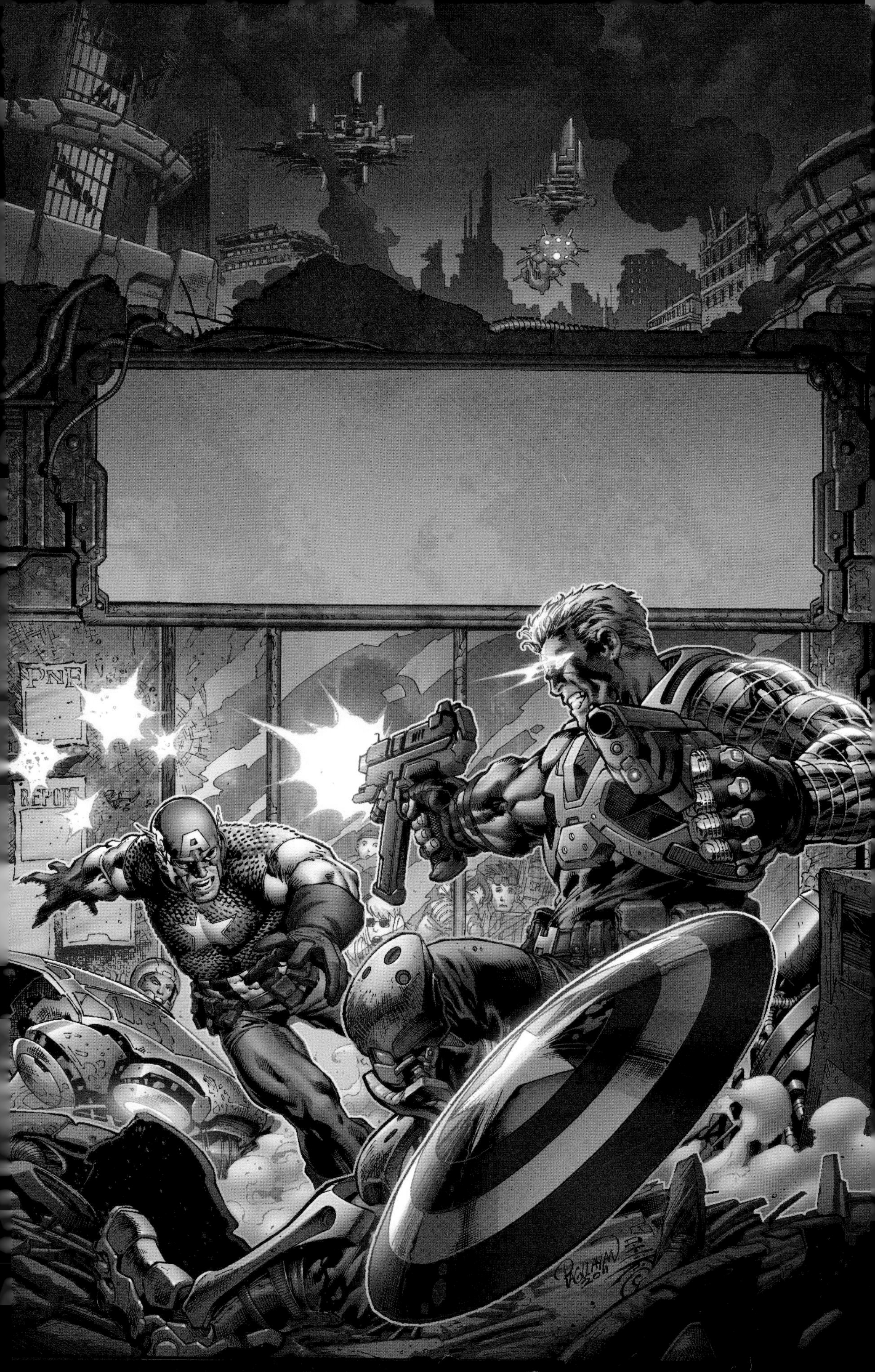
PNF
REPORT
PAGULAYAN 2011

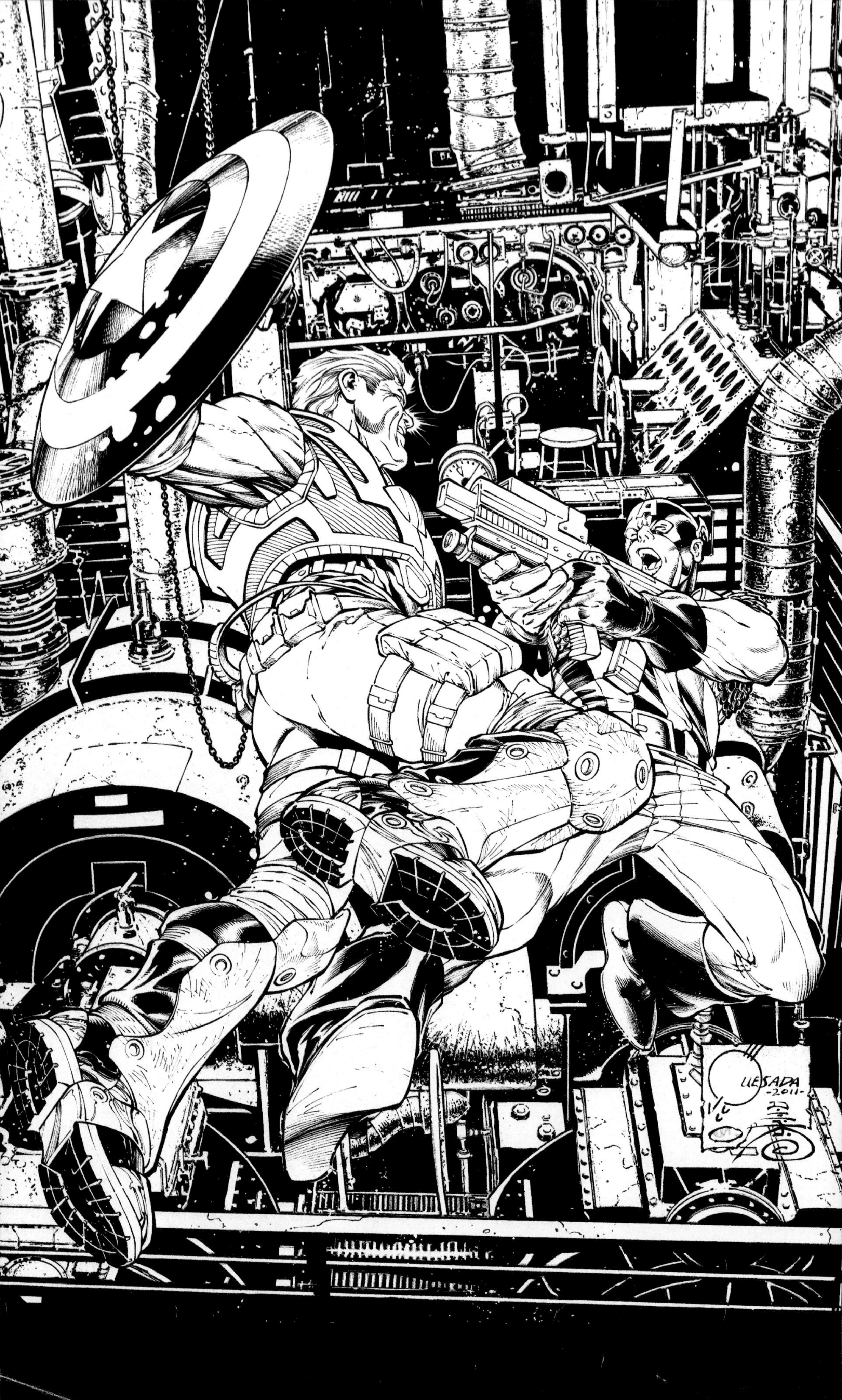

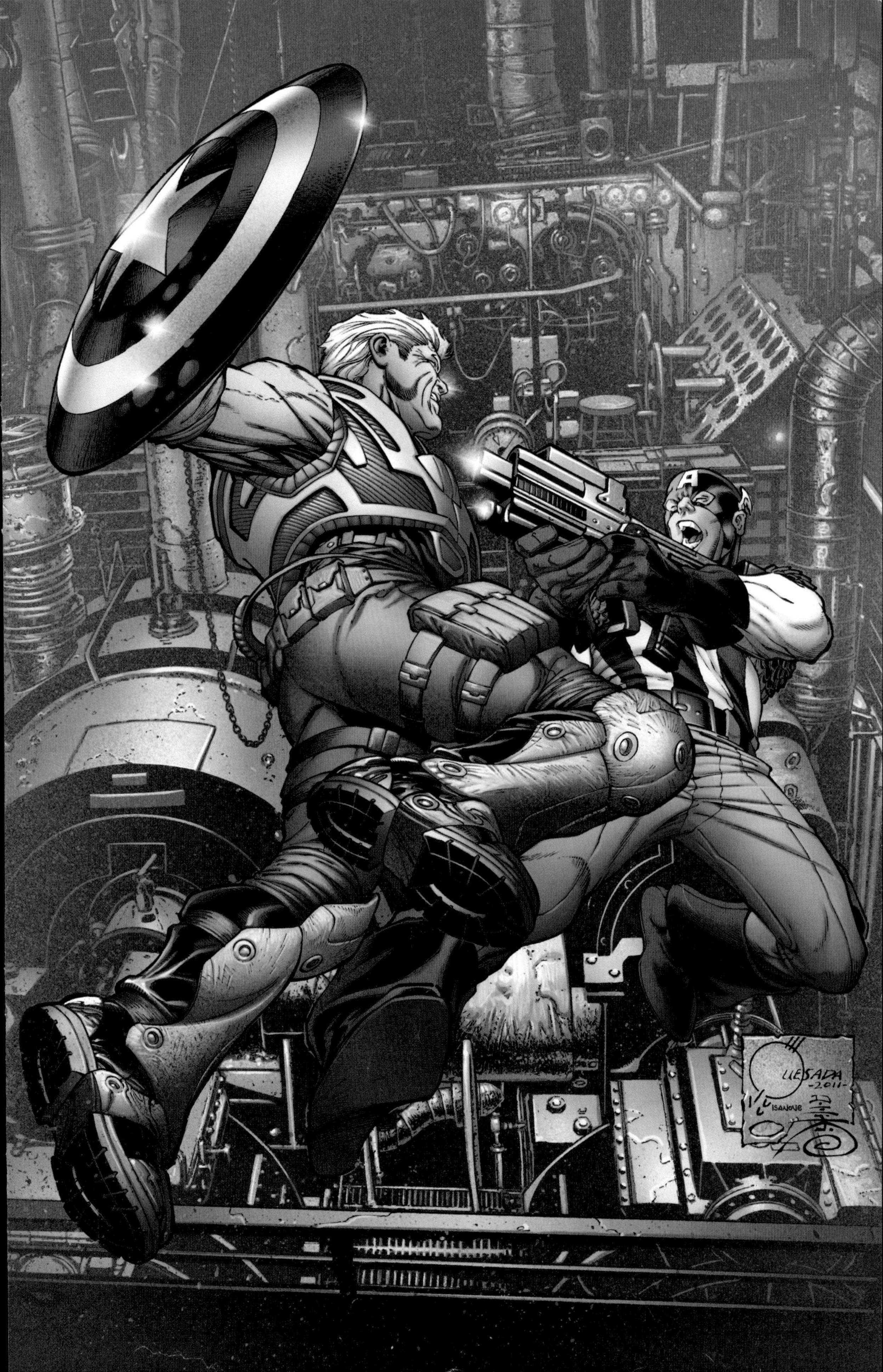

SSUE 1 VARIANT COVERS > JOE QUESADA/DANNY MIKI/RICHARD ISANOVE

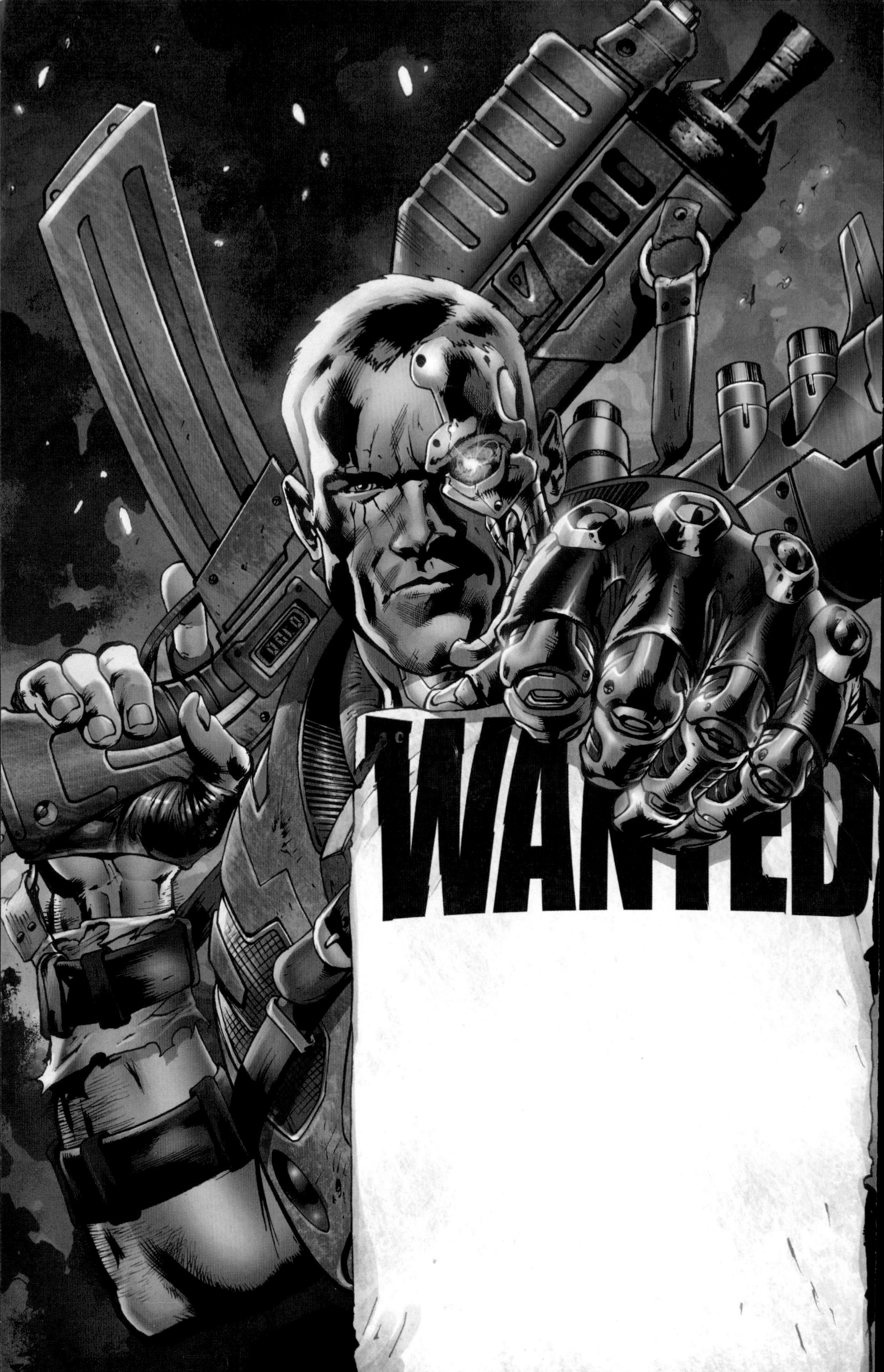
WANTED

ISSUE 1 INCENTIVE COVER > BRYAN HITCH/PAUL NEARY/PAUL MOUNT

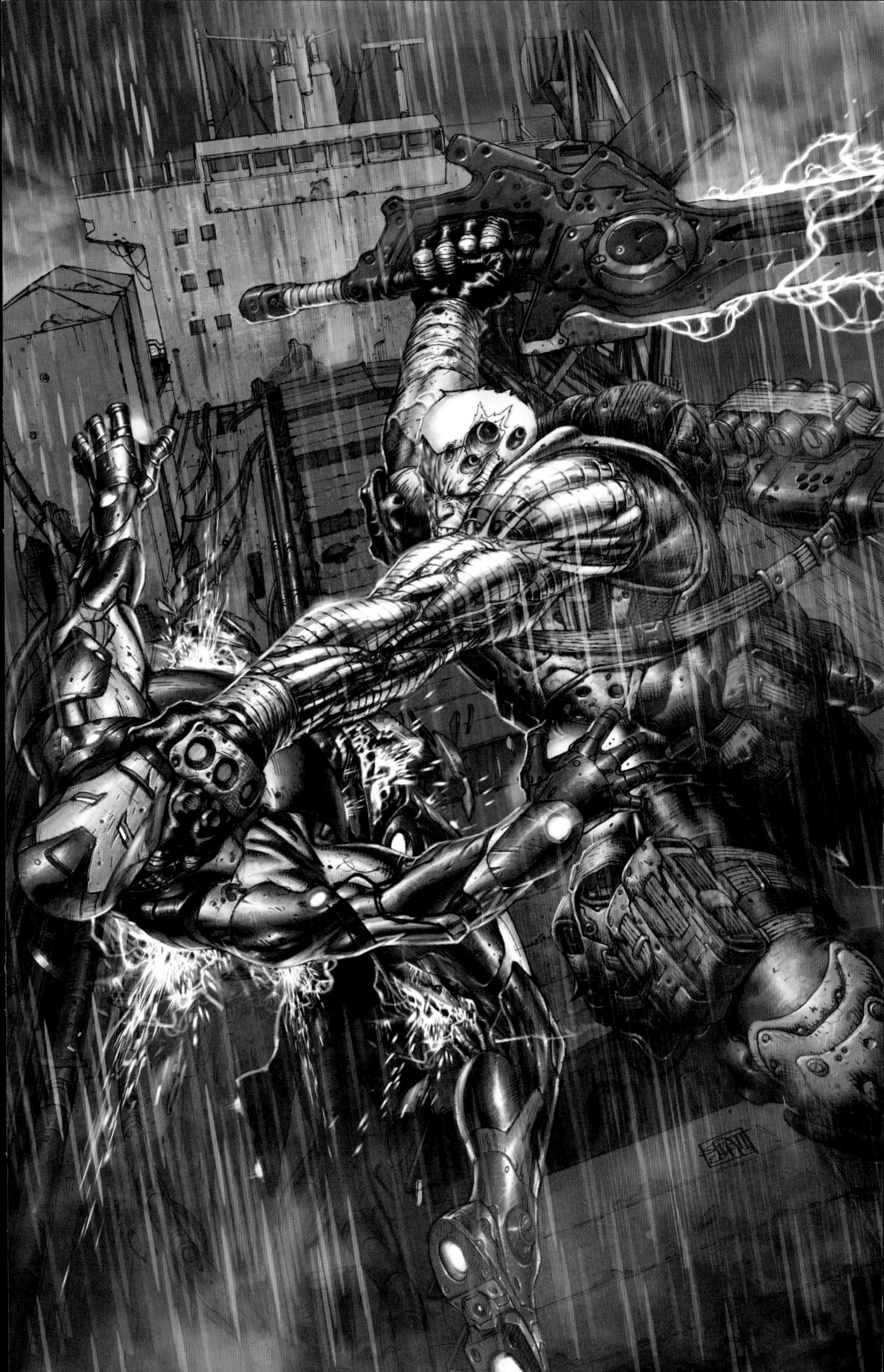

ISSUE 2 VARIANT COVER > STEPHEN PLATT

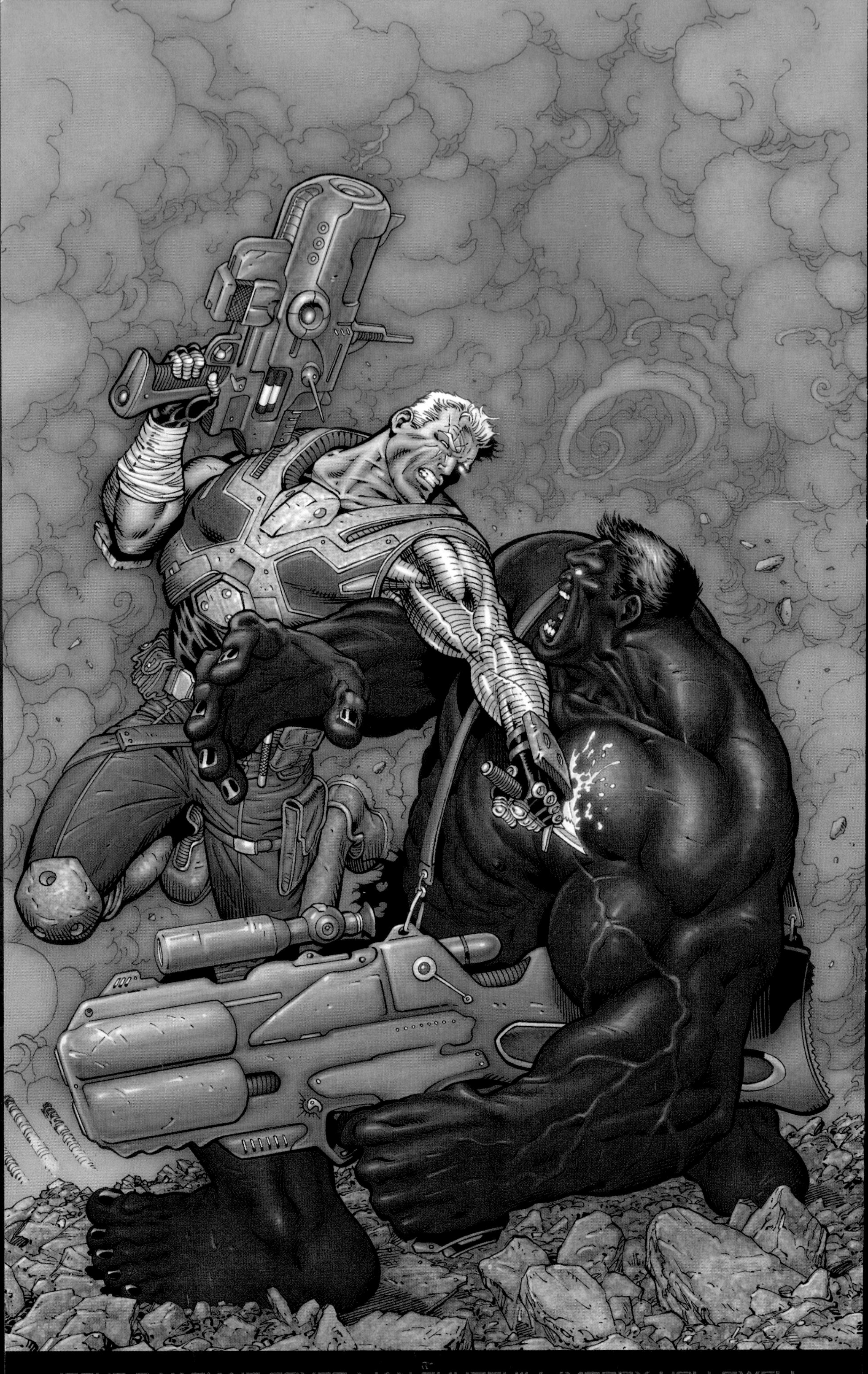

ISSUE 3 VARIANT COVER > IAN CHURCHILL/MORRY HOLLOWELL

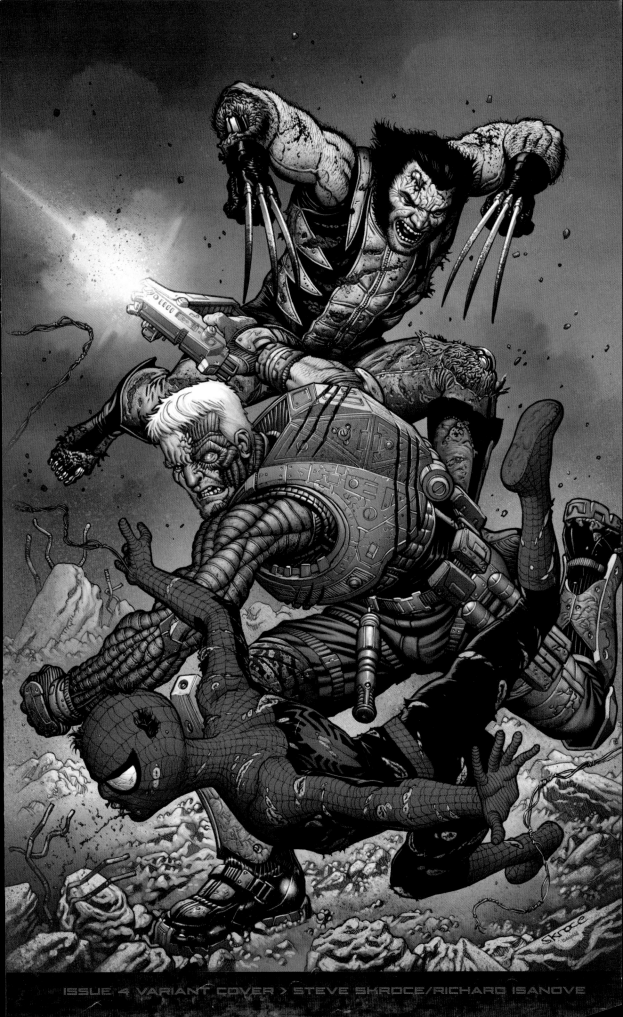

ISSUE 4 VARIANT COVER > STEVE SKROCE/RICHARD ISANOVE

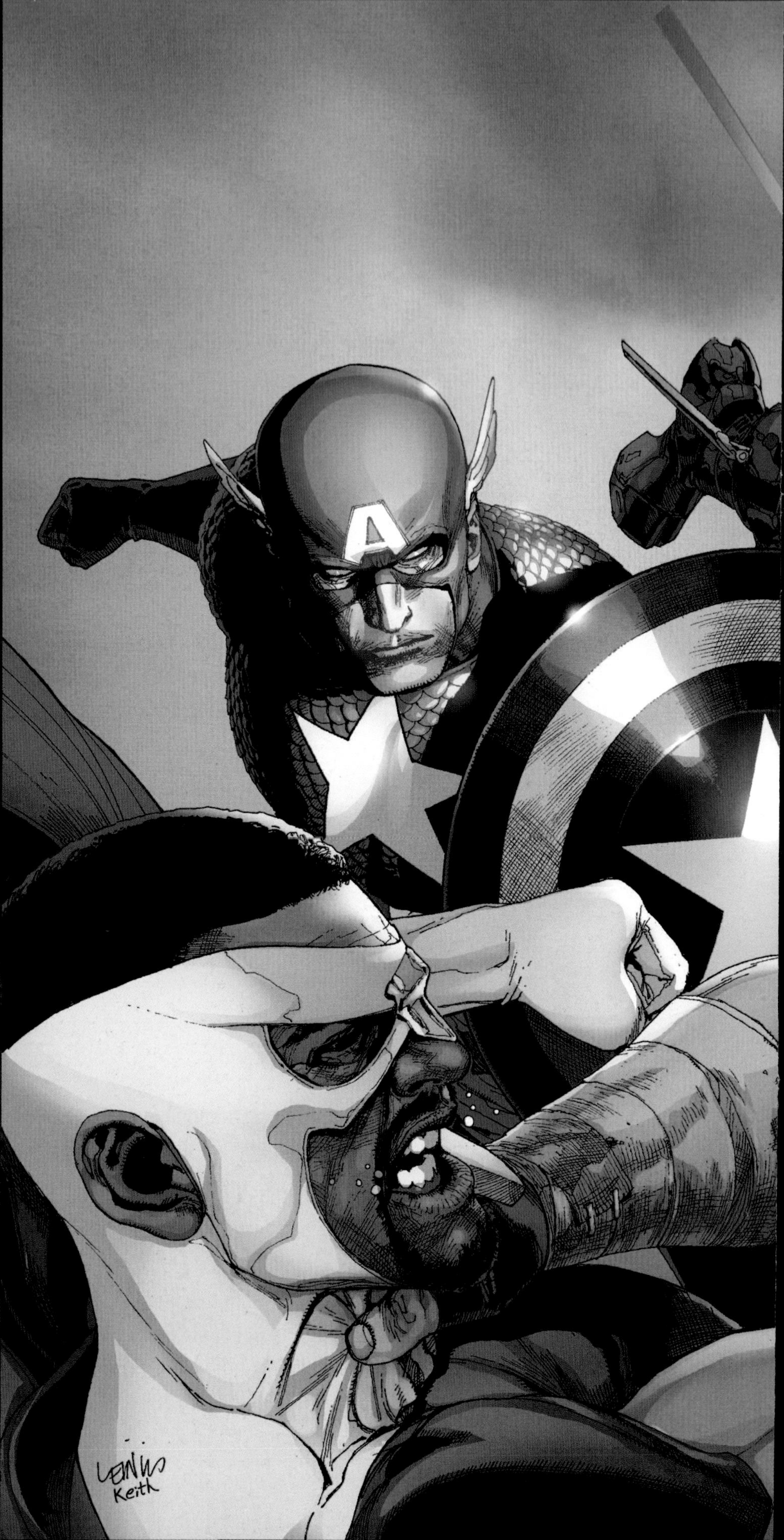

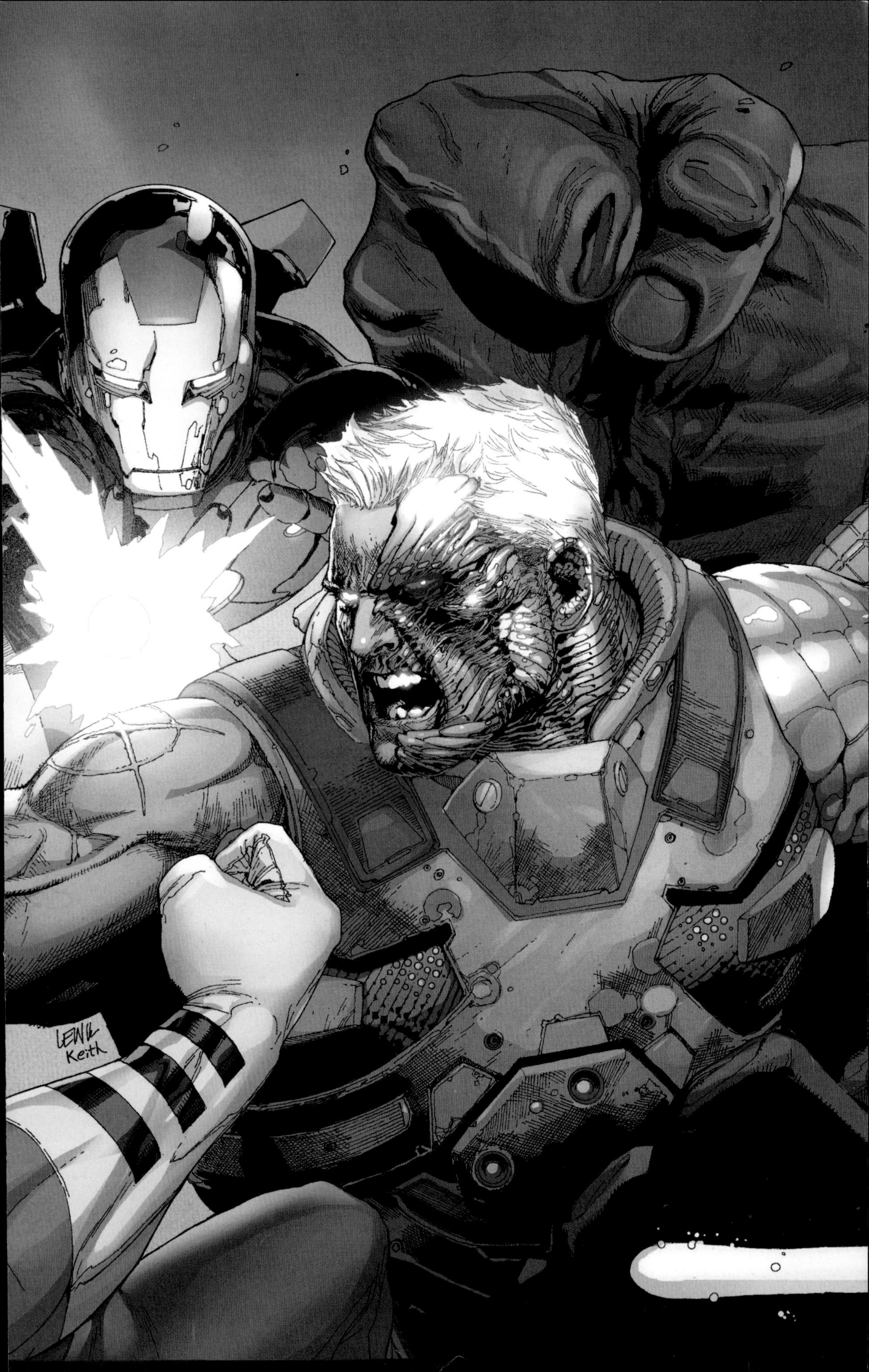
LEINIL
Keith

ISSUES 1-4 COMBINED VARIANT COVERS >
LEINIL FRANCIS YU/GERRY ALANGUILAN/JASON KEITH

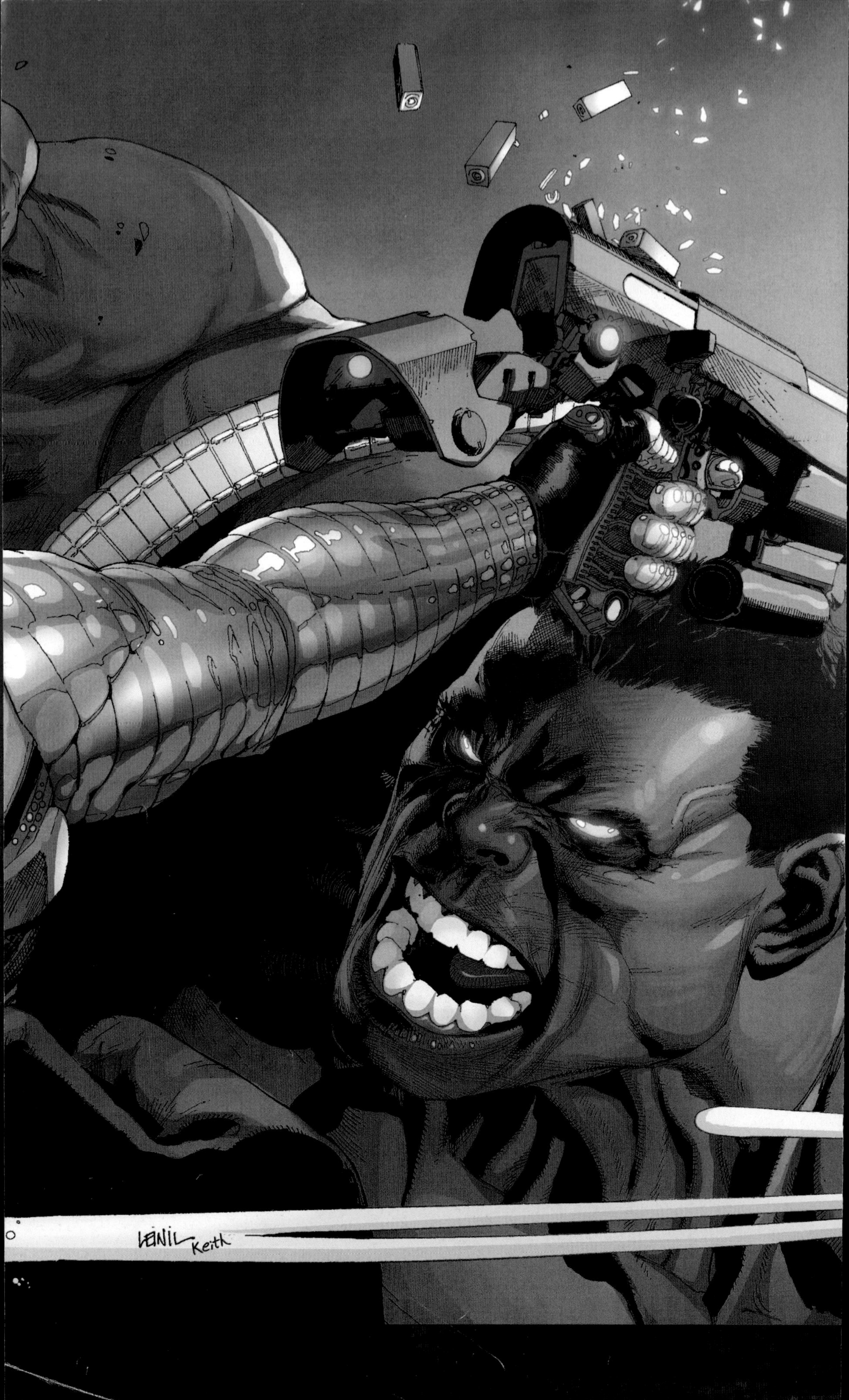
LEINIL
Keith

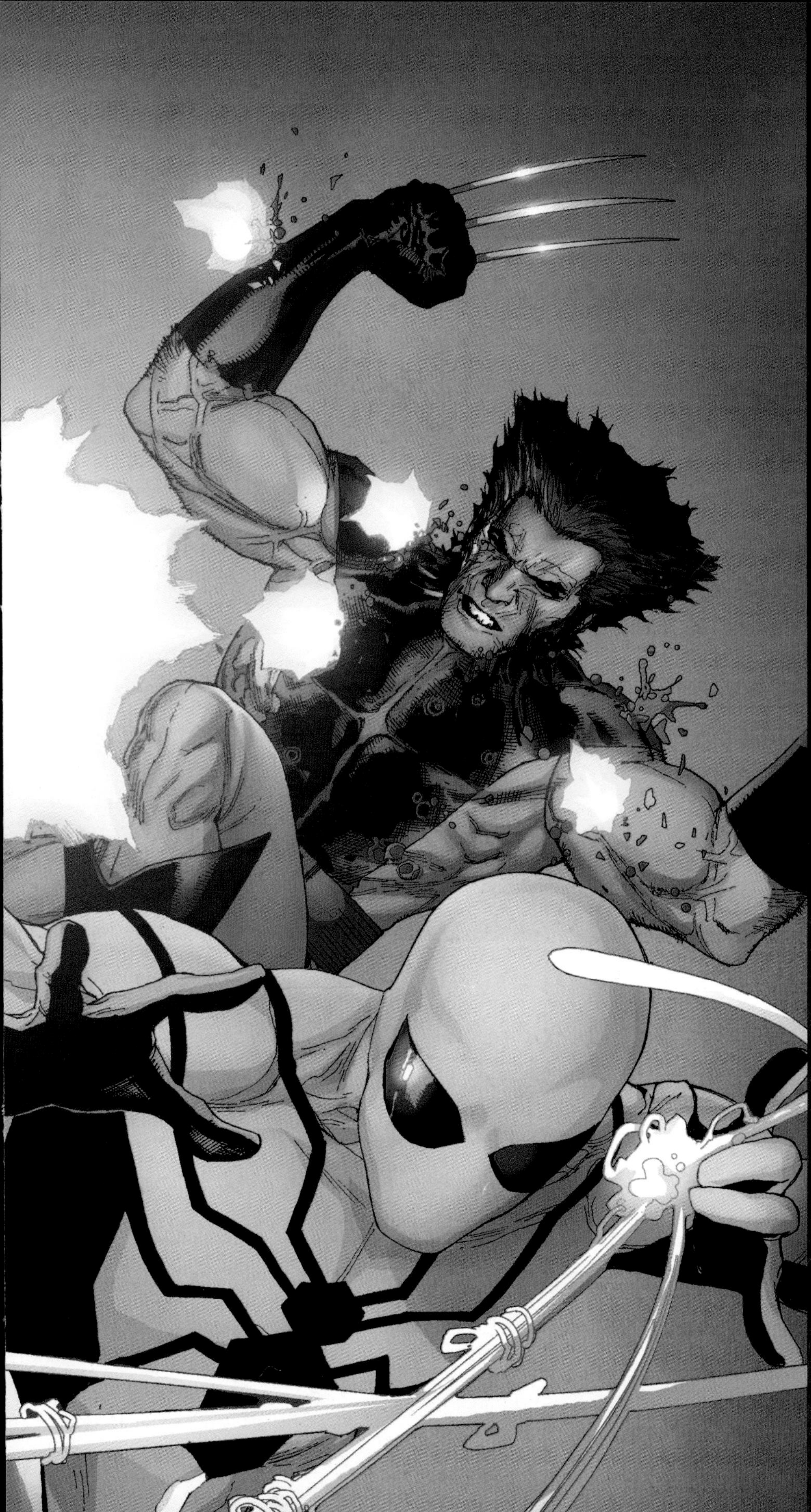

CABLE'S HAIR BECOMES BLACKER
AS THE VIRUS SPREADS.
AN IRONY TO THE STORY
TITLES.

THIN RIB
METAL - RE
WIRE MO
THE SUR
VEINS.

JEPH LOEB ›

Before we begin any
project, Ed and I talk
about the character
and what we're trying
to convey in the story.
For this, Ed wanted
to be able to redesign
Cable a bit, largely
due to the need to
show his body was
going to be covered in
technovirus and still
maintain the power of
a war-beaten soldier.

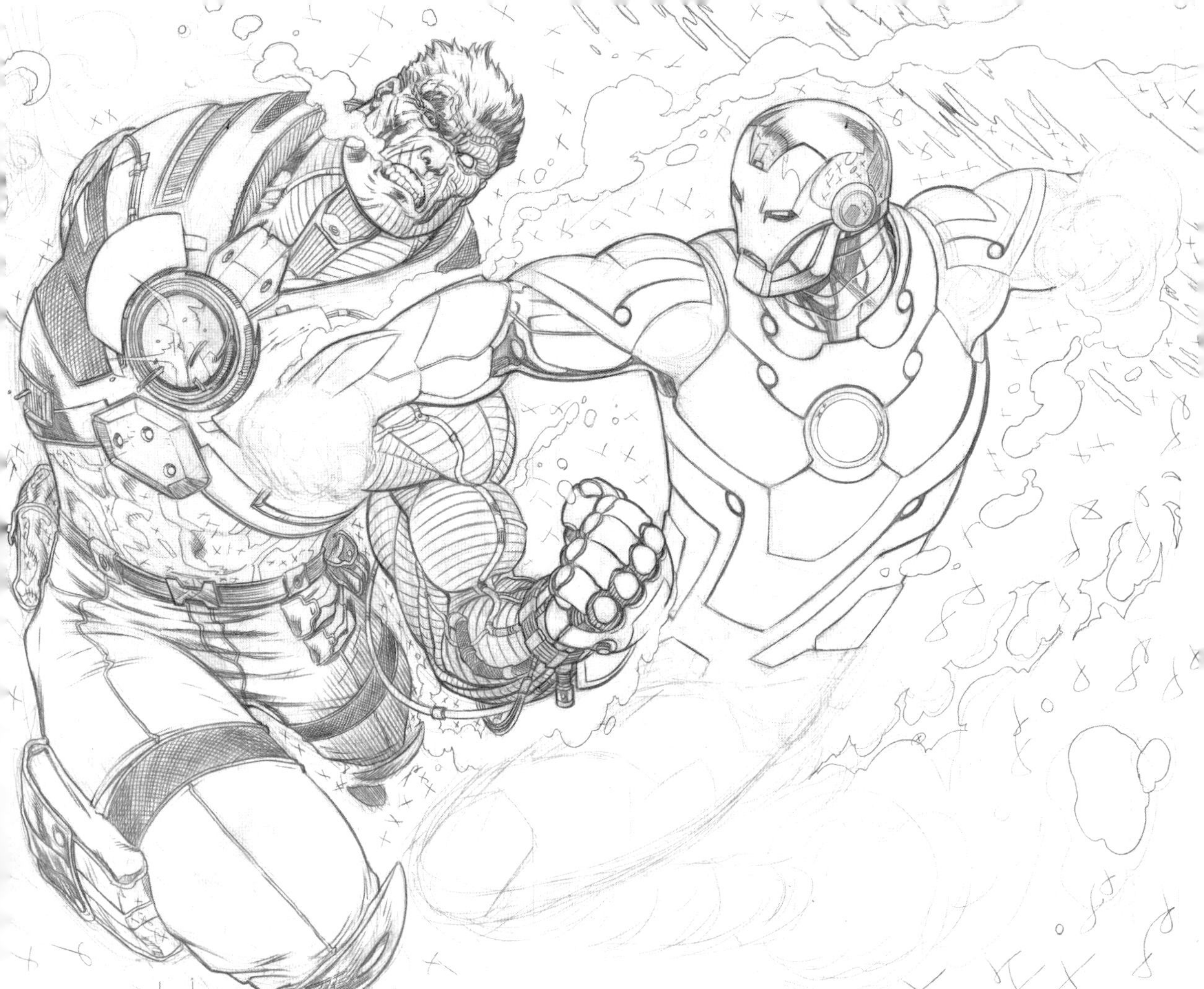

ED McGUINNESS >

SKETCHBOOK

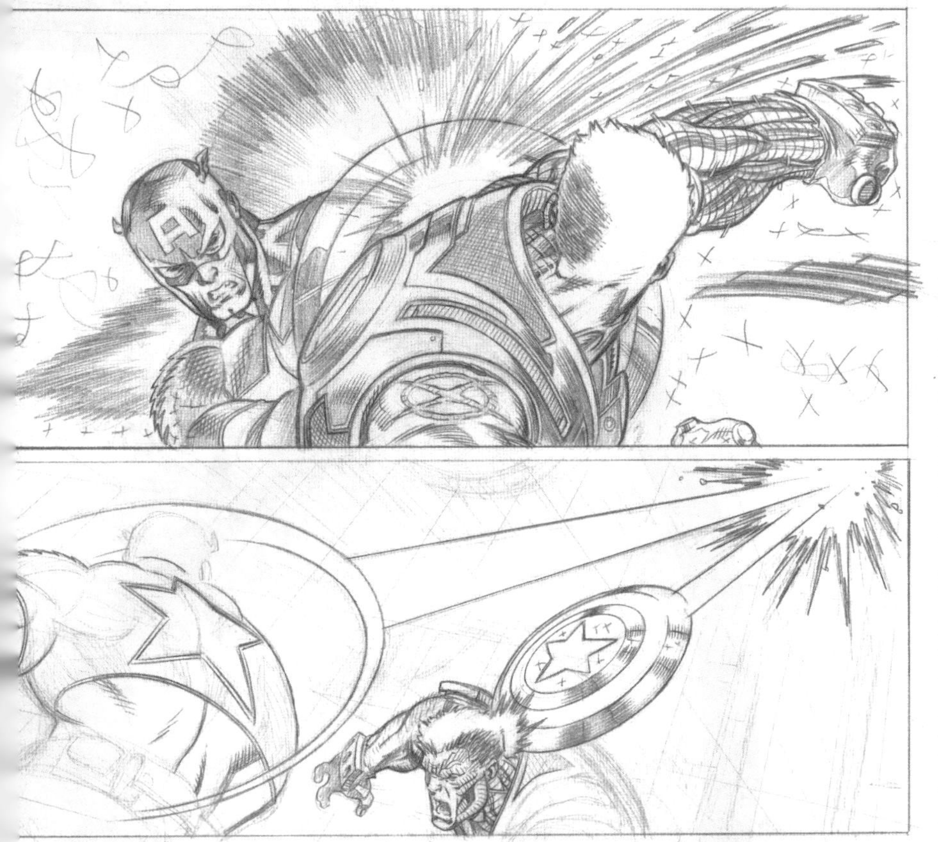

JL > One of the many joys of working with Ed is that he has that distinctive Marvel DNA in his blood. He draws pages with so much action that it can't be contained to the page -- you think that Cap's shield is going to come bouncing out of the comic itself and hit YOU!

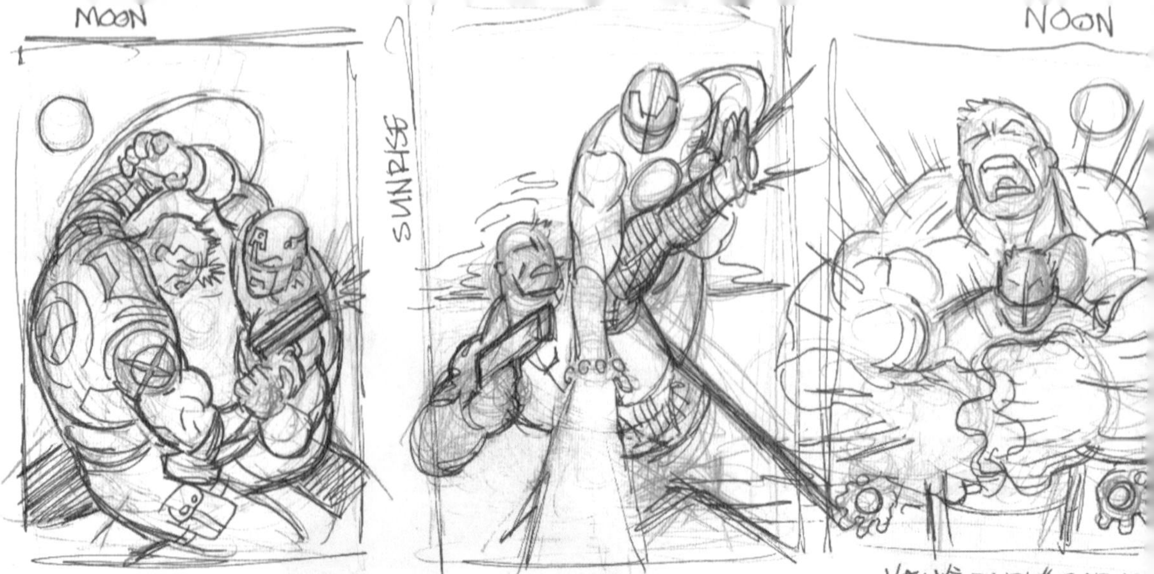
MOON
SUNRISE
NOON

- CABLE GRABBING CAP'S SHIELD ARM
- CAP GRABBING CABLE'S GUN ARM AS A SHOT GOES OFF

NOT TOO MUCH OF CABLE'S CONDITION REVEALED.

CABLE AND IRONMAN EXCHANGING REPULSOR RAYS

VERY "DARK" CABLE IMPALING RED WITH HUNDREDS OF T-VIRUS NEEDLES

GLOWING REPULSO LEFT OVER FROM I FIGHT

JL > In discussing the covers, Ed had the idea that they should be simple, iconic battles but with backgrounds that conveyed the lapsing of time since the story takes place over 18-24 hours. So we needed a horizon line, one way or the other, to show night, dawn, noon and sunset. Morry Hollowell, our astonishing colorist, brought the fire to every one of them.

VERY DARK, SHADOWY, SCAR CABLE

HARD RAIN!

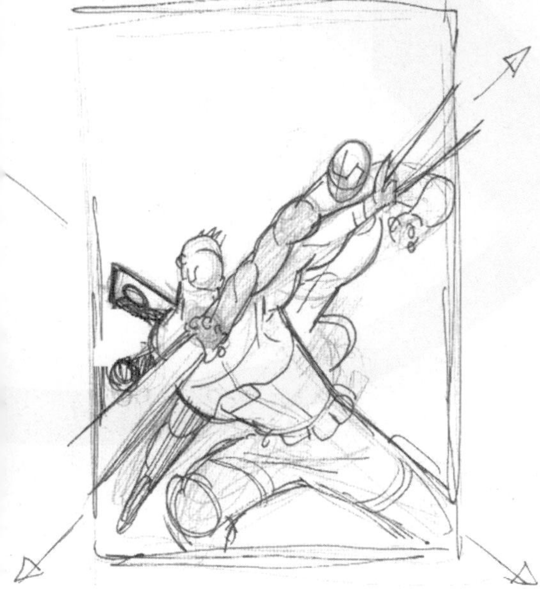

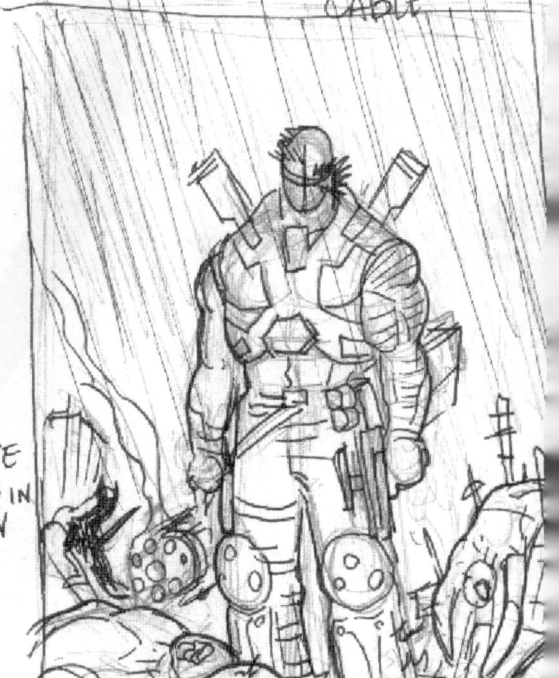

WOLVIE IMPALED IN SHADOW

HULK'S MOUTH SMOKING

BULLET HOLES IN CAP'S ARMOR

IRON MAN'S HEAD TW BACKWAR

JL > Ed reconceived the cover of issue #2 to put on the subtle "X" in their battle -- it's stuff like that where Ed's designs skills shine.

$. I THINK THIS SHOULD FEEL BRUTAL W/OUT GORE!

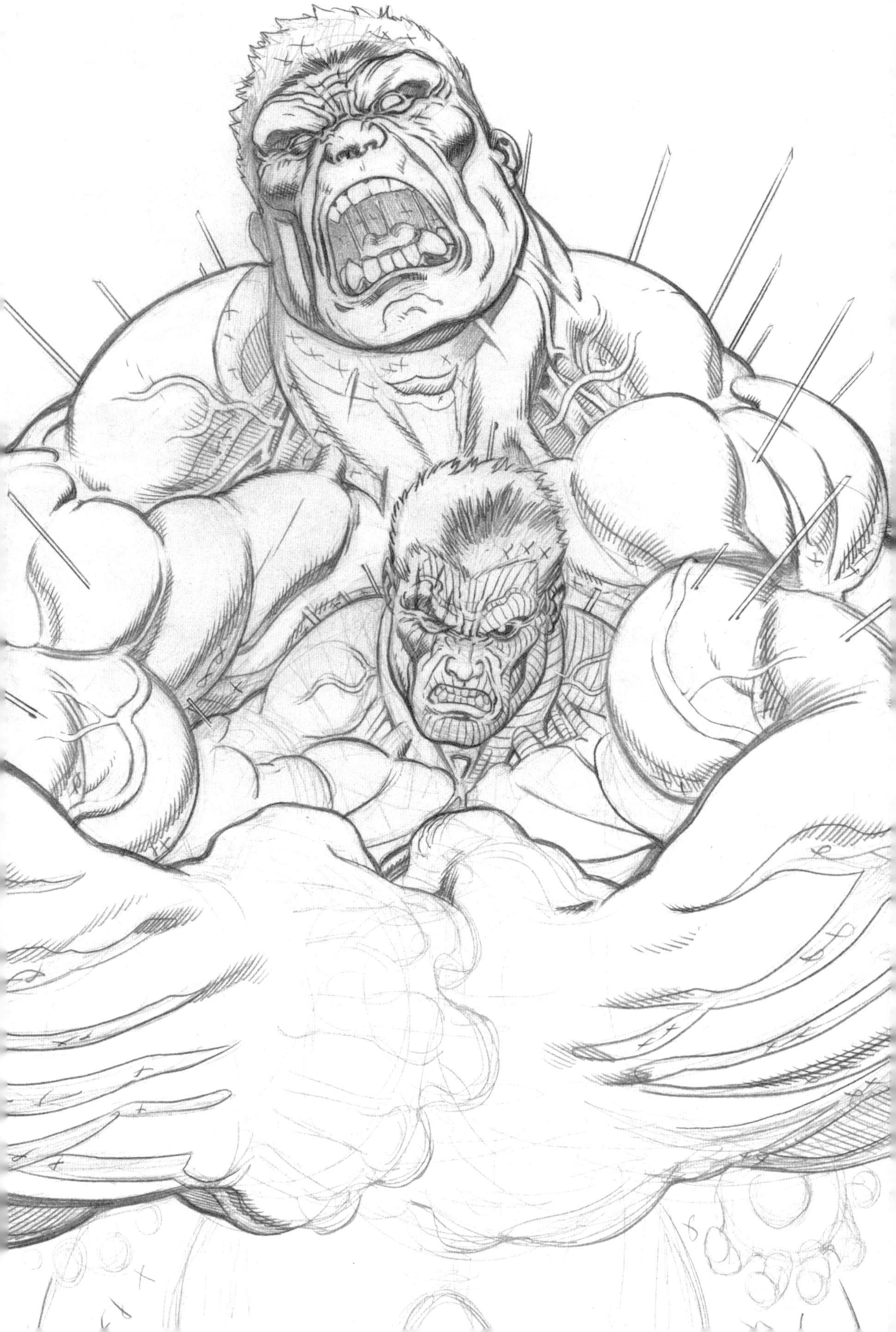

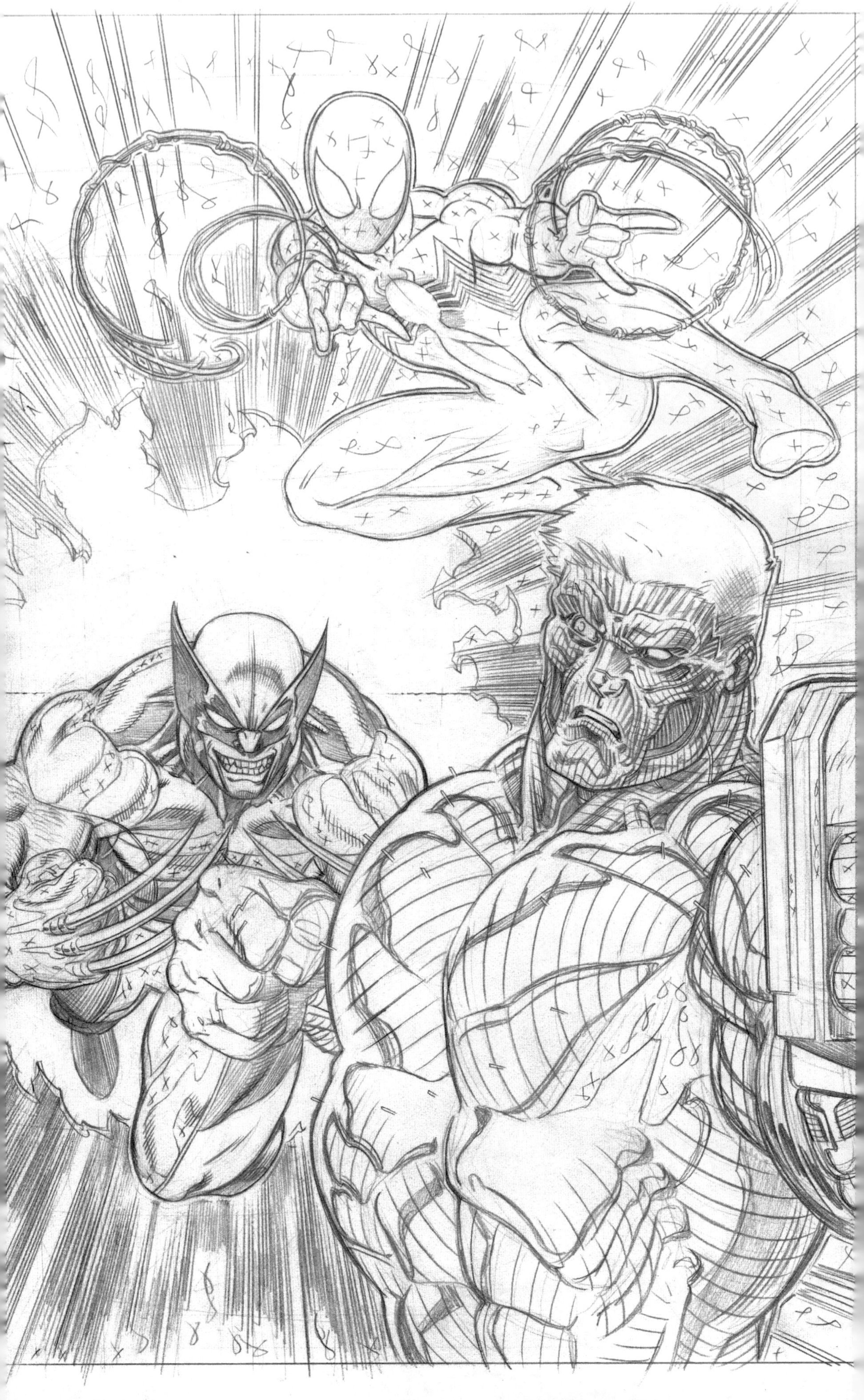

ED McGUINNESS > SKETCHBOOK

JL > On the left is one those pages you rarely get to see. From the very beginning, Ed had wanted to get Wolverine into his X-Force costume and Spidey into the black costume -- for no other reason than he loves those designs. I tried my best to make it work within the story -- even so much as to write the final page of Issue 3 with them changed. But when I started the script for Issue 4, this plot thread kept dangling and it was going to take away from the urgency of the story. The Avengers have been kidnapped, the clock is ticking, but these two heroes have time to change costumes?

Finally, I talked to Ed and he agreed, but then he had to redraw the last page of Issue #3, which fortunately had not been inked yet. The cover for Issue 4, on the other hand, was already done and solicited, so that couldn't be changed.

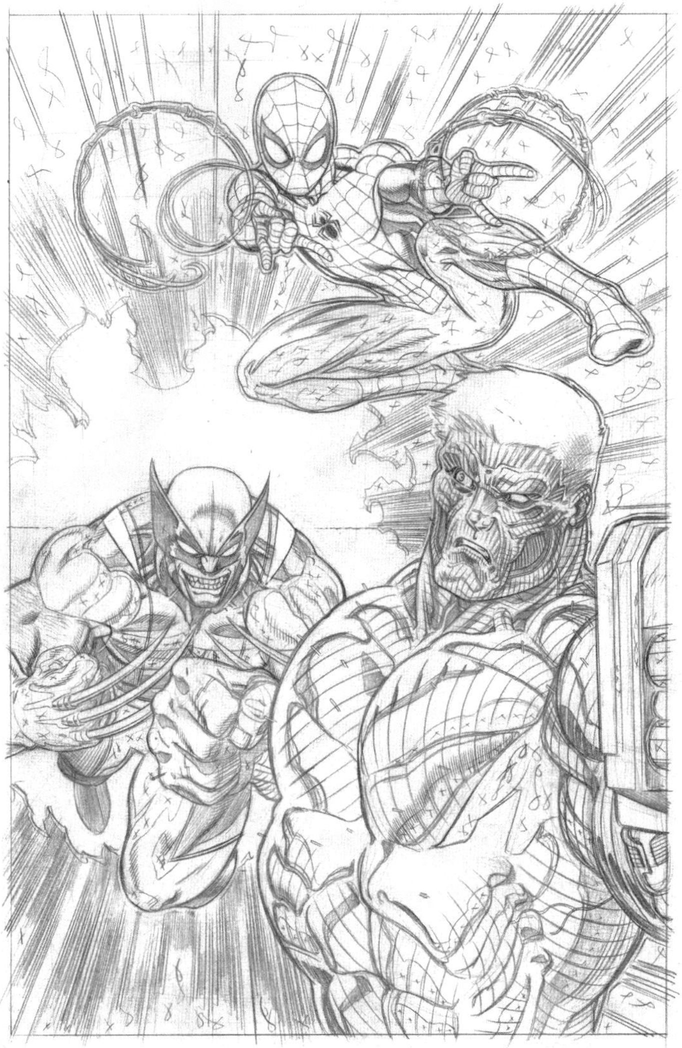

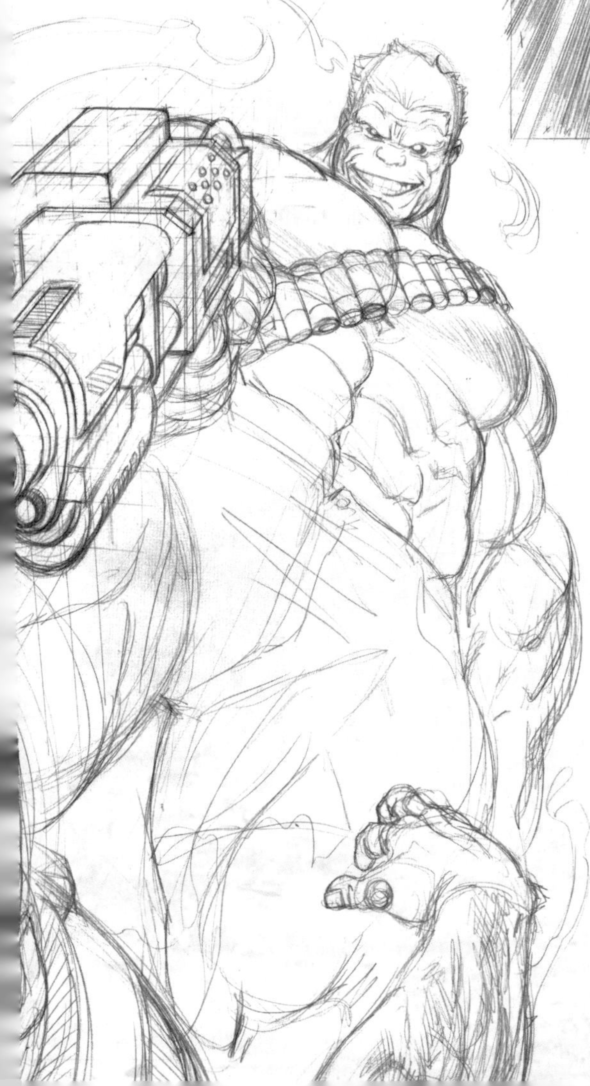

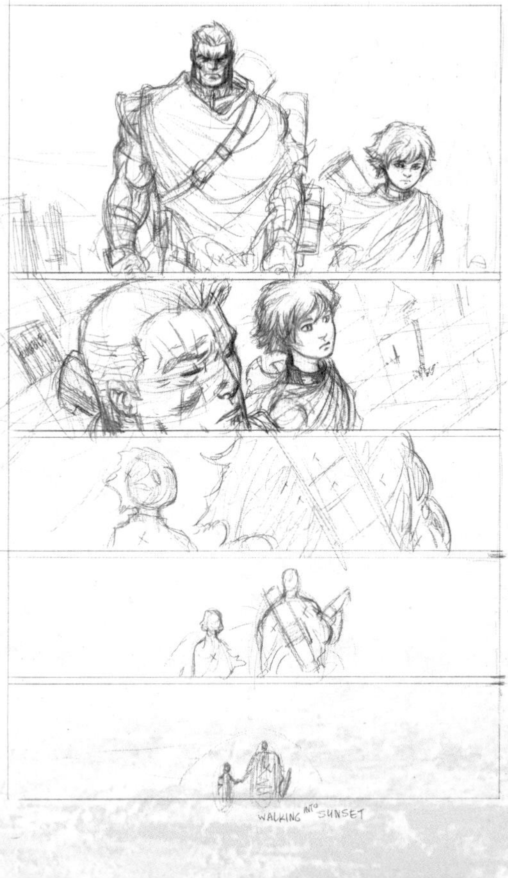
WALKING INTO SUNSET

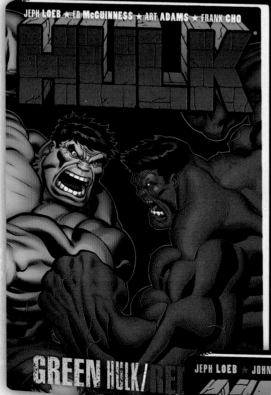
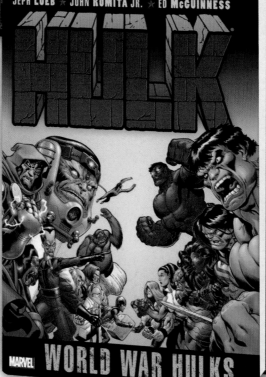